On the road with
Plantin
Travel in the 16th century

Werner van Hoof (ed.)

Gerrit Verhoeven
Dirk Imhof
Cédric Raskin
Christophe Schellekens
Hubert Meeus
Jan Papy

Museum Plantin-Moretus | Prentenkabinet

BAI

CONTENTS

4   Foreword
—
Nabilla Ait Daoud

8   Plodding Along in Plantin's Time
Travelling in the 16th century
—
Gerrit Verhoeven

26   Plantin, a Publisher Forever on the Road
—
Dirk Imhof

42   In Plantin's Footsteps
—
Cédric Raskin

76   Mobility and Stability
Jost Amman's representation of trade, transport and travel in the early modern period
—
Christophe Schellekens

92   A 16th-century Journey Planner
—
Hubert Meeus

106   Advice for Travellers by the Humanist Justus Lipsius:
Italy or "Rome n'est plus Rome"?
—
Jan Papy

124   Colophon

FOREWORD

—
Nabilla Ait Daoud
City of Antwerp Alderman for Culture

2020 was the five hundredth anniversary of Christophe Plantin's birth. Plantin was born in Saint-Avertin near Tours and settled in Antwerp in around 1550. Antwerp gave him everything he needed to set up a successful printing firm: materials, craftsmen *and* customers. Plantin expanded his *Officina Plantiniana* (Plantin Press) to become one of the most important publishing businesses in Europe.

Christophe Plantin printed books that helped shape the world: the first Dutch dictionary, atlases by Ortelius, botanical works by Dodoens, Clusius and Lobelius, and treatises by Simon Stevin. His printing office was a crossroads of knowledge and science, and a meeting point for scholars across all of Europe. Plantin did not limit his work solely to Antwerp. He also had a shop in Paris and a second printing office in Leiden. Moreover, he owned a pied-à-terre in Frankfurt. And he exported his books to every corner of Europe, as well as to North Africa and the Spanish colonies.

Plantin was successful because he was far more than just a publisher. Above all he was an ambitious, tenacious businessman. As the firm's director, he understood how to motivate his employees to deliver their best work. He had a nose for the innovations of his age – not only those relating to the book trade. Plantin knew many influential people throughout Europe, and the success of his business owed itself in no small part to his contacts. He corresponded continually with friend and foe alike, but every so often a 16th century publisher still had to meet with his patrons, suppliers, customers and authors in the flesh. Consequently, he was compelled to travel with regularity.

For many Europeans, travel since the Second World War has become synonymous with relaxation and holidays. Things were quite different in the 16th century. To set out on a journey was to enter a lion's den of perils and there had to be a good reason for leaving home. It was no less the case for Plantin. His travel bags were ever ready for yet another journey in the interests of his business or – if only temporarily – in order to avoid political and religious conflicts. Family, too, was another good reason for taking to the road.

This book attempts to sketch a picture of travel in the 16th century. Who might you meet on your journey, and just how did people travel? What do we know about Plantin's journeys? Where did he go and with whom did he speak on the way? How were these business trips organized? What about travel guidebooks? What were they like? The humanist and prominent Plantin Press author Justus Lipsius provided travel advice for anyone visiting Rome. Today's travellers can still benefit from his words. Lastly, a pictorial essay gives a photographer's contemporary interpretation of the routes between Antwerp and, respectively, Paris, Leiden and Frankfurt; he muses: 'Can we chase after the past?'

In the words of the Chinese philosopher Confucius: 'It's better to travel one mile than to read a thousand books'. Would Plantin have agreed with that? It's doubtful. He was too much the publisher and businessman; besides, travel in the 16th century was too demanding and risky. Still, our aim in this publication is to reconcile the two: travel and books. So, whether you're embarking on this book somewhere on your travels or in the comfort of your home, we wish you a pleasant journey and a highly enjoyable read.

Advice for Travellers[*]

—

"In the first place, as euery man in any course of life, so most of all a Traueller, who is subiect to many dangers, must by his daily prayers sollicite God for his gracious protection."

"Let each Traueller forecast with himselfe his owne purposes and ends. [...] I professe to write especially in this place to the Humanist, I meane him that affects the knowledge of State affaires, Histories, Cosmography, and the like, and out of that I write, let other men apply to their vse, what they iudge fit for them. And if the Humanist iudge many things I shall write lesse necessary for him, let him know, that as an Orator and Poet must haue some skill in all Sciences, so the Humanist must haue some knowledge of all things which fall into practice and discourse."

[*] The Englishman Fynes Moryson (1566–1630) travelled widely through Europe and the Holy Land. His reports provide a fascinating insight into travel in the 16th century. The quotes come from his Itinerary. Part III, Book I, Chapter II: Of Precepts for Travellers, which may instruct the vnexperienced.

Plodding Along in Plantin's Time
Travelling in the 16th century

—

Gerrit Verhoeven
Postdoctoral fellow in cultural history, University of Antwerp

> " Tout le malheur de l'homme vient d'une seule chose, qui est de ne savoir demeurer en repos dans un chambre "[1]

Although philosophers were not always advocates of travel – as demonstrated in the above quote by the French sage Blaise Pascal – society in the early modern period was exceptionally mobile. Christophe Plantin was far from an exception in that regard. The fact is that hordes of people embarked on journeys in the 16th century: pilgrims set off for Rome, Santiago de Compostela or Jerusalem, merchants roamed the important trade fairs, diplomats travelled to distant courts, and artisans wandered about in search of work, while an eclectic mix of artists, scholars and students also sallied forth. This reality is often at odds with the clichéd view of a sedentary society, which we attach too readily to the early modern period.[2] Nevertheless, what did all this travelling actually entail in practice? Who were these people setting forth on journeys in the 16th century, and why did they do it? What was it that commonly motivated people? After firstly outlining a comprehensive group portrait of the travellers, we shall then turn our attention to the practical aspects of travel. How was a journey organized in terms of transport, lodgings and finance? How did travellers come by information in foreign parts? Finally, we shall also take a moment to consult the map. Which destinations were considered *vaut-le-voyage* in the 16th century? Which regions did people prefer to avoid? To answer these questions, historians have delved into a deep and wide-ranging pool of source material. Personal travel journals and letters, diplomas from foreign universities, receipts and invoices, travellers' guidebooks, and numerous other sources all shed some light on the matter, allowing us to reconstruct these experiences of travel from the historical past.

Who – *a profile of 16th-century travellers*

Literally thousands of early modern pilgrims had their names recorded in the rolls kept at San Giuliano dei Fiamminghi (the Church of St. Julian of the Flemings) in Rome, where, for centuries, pilgrims from the Low Countries had found a safe haven. Following their long journey, this was where they were given three days' lodging. Although, originally, pilgrimages had been a medieval phenomenon, the practice continued to enjoy great popularity in the 16th and 17th centuries as well. The faithful set forth to atone for their sins, either to secure plenary indulgences or to supplicate for cures, as demonstrated by the countless *ex votos* on which the afflicted bodily parts or limbs – eyes, ears, lips, arms and legs – were depicted. In addition

01 A man and woman welcoming some pilgrims. Crispijn I de Passe (engraver); after Maerten de Vos; Adriaen Collaert (publisher), *Hosting the Homeless*, 1590–1637.
Museum Plantin-Moretus, PK.OP.11944

02 David I Teniers (engraver), *Pilgrim*. Museum Plantin-Moretus, PK.OP.03105

to Rome, Santiago de Compostela and Jerusalem, regional sites of pilgrimage such as Halle, Scherpenheuvel, Kevelaer or Cologne also lured a flood of visitors. After the Reformation, there was a large-scale downturn in the numbers of Protestant travellers from the Northern Netherlands, England, the German principalities and Scandinavia. However, Catholic pilgrims continued faithfully travelling to Rome, Loreto or Turin. It was only in the late 17th century that this popularity began to wane, with the number of guests at San Giuliano falling sharply – and thus the number of pilgrims as well. In actual fact, pilgrims were not always motivated for purely religious reasons. Venice, for example, from whence northern Europeans had traditionally embarked for the Holy Land, was also much favoured because of its incomparable art treasures at St. Mark's Basilica and the Doge's Palace, its luxury businesses at the Rialto Bridge and its spectacular festivities during the annual carnival.[3]

As well as pilgrims, there were also artisans lodging at San Giuliano. Weavers, coopers, carpenters, masons, rope-makers and other craftsmen often traversed multiple countries and regions in search of work. In France, a 'tour' taking in the principal centres of production would even constitute an intrinsic part of the process that led to becoming a master craftsman. In other words, mobility was essential. Artisans and artists were also recruited by royal and ecclesiastical clients ready to pay good money for quality. For example, tapestry weavers, stained-glass artists, organists, sculptors and other masters from Flanders found the pope to be a generous patron and would reside in Rome for varying lengths of time. Likewise, Frans Floris, Pieter Bruegel the Elder, Maerten de Vos and Peter Paul Rubens also travelled to Italy to hone their technique, to scoop up lucrative commissions or to behold the masters of the Renaissance at first hand. Travelling was equally indispensable for merchants and bankers, who regularly went on the road to forge new trading ties, to settle debts or to sell their wares at trade fairs. For example, publishers and printers from across Europe held annual *rendez-vous* at the Frankfurt and Leipzig Trade Fairs. Plantin and

03 Hans Bol (engraver),
Robbery in a Wood, 1550–1593.
Museum Plantin-Moretus, PK.OP.00071

his descendants were in regular attendance.[4] Owing to the difficulty of communication by post and the lack of international trading rules, travelling was often a necessary evil for businesses such as the *Officina Plantiniana* which had many contacts abroad. Ordering or supplying books in good faith was a perilous undertaking when separated by hundreds of miles while never having met your trading partner in the flesh and thus not knowing their reputation either. In such cases, a short trip abroad was often the safer option. Moreover, a journey that took in along the way the principal international trading firms was frequently the culmination of prospective young traders' training – traders who, *en route*, could practise their double-entry bookkeeping, foreign languages, business administration and other practical skills. These budding businessmen would often serve a traineeship under a colleague and friend abroad. Publishers soon became aware of this new niche market and brought out specialist travel guides that provided information about exchange rates, foreign weights and measures, insurance premiums and so forth. Diplomats made equally long journeys. In 1622, the ambassador Johan Berck was dispatched to Venice. Berck did not make the long trip alone. In addition to his family, he also travelled accompanied by servants. It took several fatiguing weeks before the company finally arrived in Venice.⁵

A further motivating force emerged over the course of the 16th century, influenced this time by humanism. As the icing on the cake of their studies, the scions of illustrious noble and bourgeois families increasingly set out on educational journeys (*peregrinatio academica*) to famous universities in Italy (such as Bologna or Padua), France (Montpellier, Orléans or Paris) or Switzerland (Geneva), where – without too much difficulty – they acquired a pompous academic title. Academies that furnished practical instruction in the noble art of horse riding, fencing or conversation, also exerted a magnetic attraction on travellers from the north, who hoped such institutions would rid them of their boorish and coarse manners. Saumur, Angers, and other academies on the Loire were favourites, because it was there that the most refined forms of etiquette were in circulation and the purest form of French was spoken. Over the course of the 16th century, this *peregrinatio academica* evolved to become a veritable Grand Tour in which elite travellers would go on a (year-) long round trip through France, Italy and Switzerland. In that context, it was important above all to be immersed in the world of

04 Jan I Brueghel, *A Cart on a Country Road*, 1589–1626.
   Museum Plantin-Moretus, PK.OT.00226

05 Peeter Baltens, *Robbery in the Woods*, 1541–1589.
Museum Plantin-Moretus, PK.OT.00004

Classical Antiquity and – preferably with works by Vergil, Tacitus or some other authority to hand – to visit famous sites that had played a part in Roman history, such as the Roman Forum and the Colosseum, the Rubicon, Lake Trasimeno or the Crypta Neapolitana. At the same time, these Grand Tour travellers would also visit collections where they could stare in wonder at Greek and Roman sculpture, ancient illuminated manuscripts, gemstones, corals and other natural curiosities, Renaissance masterpieces, and numerous other works of art.[6] Letters sent back to the home front reveal how this experience was not always one where lofty humanist ideals reigned supreme. In 1607, the tutor to Willem and Reinier van Oldenbarnevelt complained bitterly that his pupils were seriously misbehaving on their Grand Tour, spending their days gambling, carousing and whoring, while neglecting their studies. Back at home, papa – Johan van Oldenbarnevelt, who was also the Lands' Advocate of Holland (chairman of the States of Holland) – was anything but amused. (See also the contribution by Jan Papy.)[7]

06 Entourage of Jan I Brueghel, *Village Scene*, 1589–1625. Museum Plantin-Moretus, PK.OT.00230

How – *a checklist of troubles en route*

Diplomats, noblemen, pilgrims, traders, artisans and students all covered hundreds of miles on their journeys, while their circumstances were often far from ideal. Roads were usually little more than primitive cart tracks through the landscape. A brief downpour in autumn or winter was typically all it took to transform them into endless rivers of mud, while travellers in the spring and summer would be grinding the thrown-up dust between their teeth. Transport opportunities were few and far between. Coaches had been running services between the major cities since the mid-16th century, but – in the absence of suspension on these deplorable roads – the experience was abominable in terms of comfort. Consequently, most travellers preferred to spend hours in the saddle, which meant a choice between your own horsepower or a hired variety. Receipts and invoices reveal that the first option brought with it a great many headaches: travellers were continually engaged in buying new reins, halters, spurs, saddles and saddlebags which were worn to shreds owing to the amount of horse riding involved; additionally, they had to dig deep in their purses to pay for stabling, fodder, horseshoes and more besides. By contrast, this made the hiring of courier horses seem a good deal simpler. At a stopover point you would hire a mount which, after only a few miles, you could exchange for a fresh steed, thus enabling you to cover a fair distance without problems. This system had arisen in 15th century Italy and since then had spread like wildfire across the rest of Europe. Barges were, by far, the safest and most comfortable means of travel, plying up and down the Loire, the Rhine, the Brenta and other major rivers.

07 Unknown. *Horses in Front of a Cart.* Museum Plantin-Moretus, PK.OT.00298

Most travellers switched effortlessly between the many transport options on offer and on their journey would combine riding on horseback or in a coach, sailing on a barge and even going on foot. The least popular itineraries were perhaps those involving voyages at sea, such as the short trip across the English Channel, the journey from Genoa to Livorno by *feluca* or the long crossing to the Holy Land. Landlubbers were invariably anxious in the face of seasickness, storms and dead calms, and privateers sailing the coast. The Mediterranean Sea had a particularly poor reputation as far as pirates were concerned. In 1585, during a sea voyage from Amsterdam to Hamburg, Plantin experienced the risks at first hand when his ship sailed into a severe storm. (See the contribution by Dirk Imhof.)[8]

Dangers lay in wait around every corner, or, that is, they did, if we are to take travellers at their word, because their journals are routinely full of tall stories about highwaymen and swindlers, spectacular accidents, and other calamities.

One route always much commented upon in journals was the perilous crossing of the Alps. Fynes Moryson, some of whose travel advice is included in this book, described his experiences in the 1590s in haunting style:

> "At times I would climb not without trepidation the steepest of mountain passes, bent over forwards, my face upon the neck of my horse, which I then gave free rein. With the one hand I held myself fast to his mane and with the other to the saddle."[9]

Given that the crossing between France and Italy over the Mont Cenis Pass was too steep for horses, travellers went by mule, by litter or – in winter – by sledge. In this terrain, those from the Low Countries would invariably break into a cold sweat. Another risk that travellers had to keep duly in mind in mountainous, densely forested or otherwise isolated regions was the possibility of becoming lost. In the absence of signposts, each fork in the road was a cause for equivocation. For that reason, numerous travellers would

08 Joannes and Lucas van Doetecum (engravers); Hans Bol (draughtsman); Hieronymus Cock (publisher), *River Landscape with a City at the Foot of a High Mountain*, 1562. (detail)
Museum Plantin-Moretus, PK.OP.15736

go accompanied by a *vetturino* or guide, who not only knew the route like the back of his hand, but could also arrange lodgings and transport along the way. For a set fee, they provided a form of all-in package whereby the traveller – more or less – could have peace of mind.[10] Travel guidebooks, of course, were also a source of information and had been appearing on the market with increasing frequency since the 16th century. For example, Charles Estienne's *La guide des chemins de France* (Paris, 1552) gave an inventory of all the postal routes in France – including stopover points and the number of miles between cities – and it also supplied information about sightseeing opportunities *en route*. Moreover, readers found within it some supplementary culinary tips about the delectable white wines of Gaillac, the delicious woodcock from Bris, the succulent capons from Loudun and other delicacies. Another "bestseller" was the *Sommaire description de la France, Allemagne, Italie & Espagne* (Geneva, 1592). (See also the contribution by Hubert Meeus.)[11]

Locating a comfortable – or at the very least, clean – inn at a reasonable price was no easy matter. Particularly in rural and less densely populated areas, travellers might not infrequently be brought down to earth with a jolt. However, even in cities there could be occasions of much sorrow and misery. Michel de Montaigne, the French philosopher and author of the *Essays*, complained vociferously about lodgings on his journey through Switzerland:

"… the beds never have curtains and always there are three of four beds to a room, one up against the other. There is no hearth; one has warmth only in the taprooms and dining halls … Lucky is he who is given a white bed sheet. It is not the custom here to cover the pillow with a pillow case. Rarely do they have bed covers other than a feather bed, and then a most filthy one at that."[12]

Moreover, communication was a continual problem, because of the misunderstandings engendered by language differences. To remedy such shortcomings, travellers purchased phrase books, such as the *Dialogues en quatre languages, françoise, espagnolle, italienne & allemande* (Amsterdam, 1656), in which all manner of situations were tackled. Readers were familiarized with an abundance of standard phrases that they could use in every conceivable circumstance: how to ask for clean sheets, to complain about a snoring bedfellow, to order soup, to scold the stable boy, to request a barber or to arrange innumerable other matters. In any case, Italian, French or German inns were ideal biotopes in which to refine one's knowledge of foreign languages; it was there that travellers from the North could finally put into practice the grammatical theory and vocabulary lessons that had been drilled into them at home.[13]

Letters also played a part in practising languages and displaying scholastic progress. This explains why young travellers would often write home in their "best" broken French or Italian, while their parents would overload them with practical advice and news from the mother country. At times these letters illustrate, too, the high emotional toll exacted by such long journeys, because correspondence often included liberal helpings of homesickness and nostalgia. That

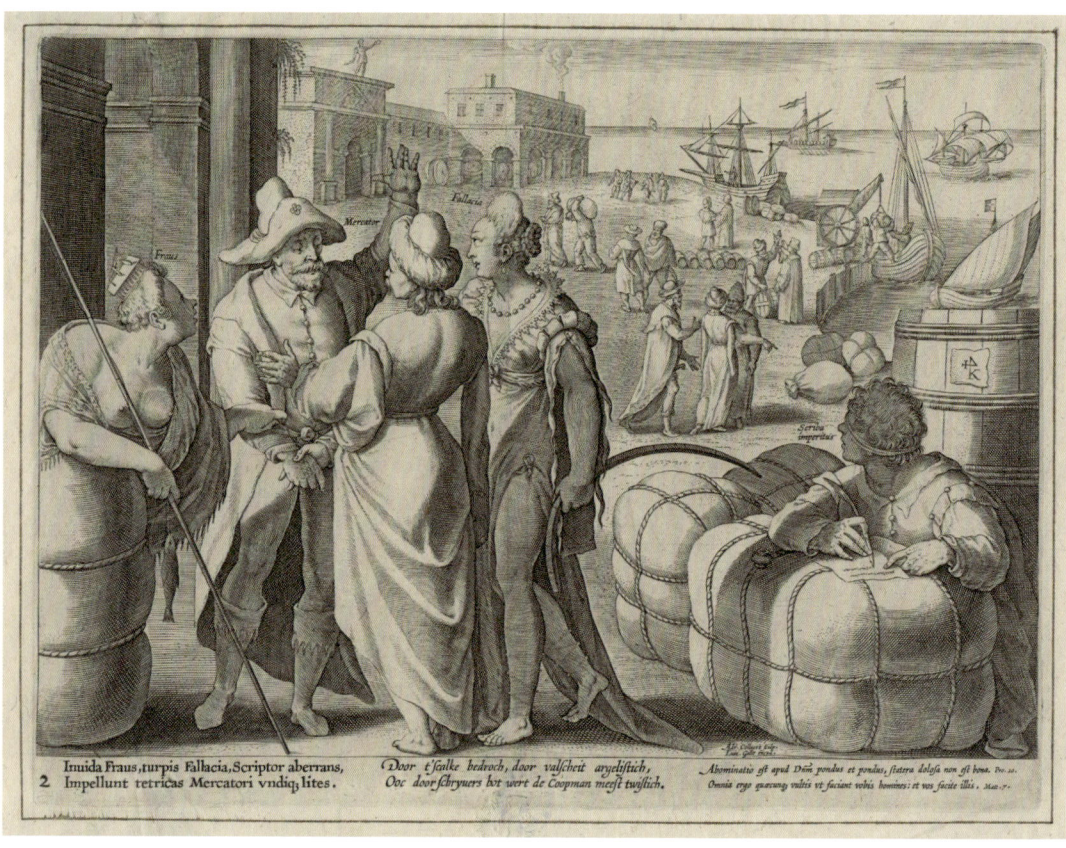

09 Adriaen Collaert (engraver); Hendrick Goltzius (draughtsman); Joannes Galle (publisher), *Quarrel owing to Commercial Deceit*, 1565–1618.
Museum Plantin-Moretus, PK.OP.12928

sense of deprivation became all the more acute if the exchange of letters should be interrupted for any reason, such as the mail having been lost *en route* or subject to a delay. Somewhat dismayed, Samuel de Bacher, the son of an Amsterdam merchant, wrote on 24 December 1610 from Venice:

> "I had hoped to find here letters from father and other friends, as well as … among those of Castro, but have found none. I am most saddened by this …"[14]

Finances were also an important topic of discussion in letters. Bacher continually begged for his travel budget to be increased, because of the high costs incurred for transport, lodgings and numerous other matters, whereas his parents were nevertheless at pains to have him tighten his purse strings. Penny-pinching quibbles of this sort were the common thread running through a great deal of correspondence.[15] Understandably, these travellers rarely if ever carried their money with them in cash. Given the number of brigands on the road, such a policy would have signed your own death warrant and, moreover, virtually every principality in Italy had its own currency, which would have meant continually having to convert one form of coinage to another. A bill of exchange to bearer was a far more practical proposition. Prior to departure, travellers would visit a local merchant with international contacts and, in exchange for a cash payment, he would write out a bill of exchange. Once in Italy or France, this paper money could be redeemed for cash again in the same manner.[16] In addition to bills of exchange, 16th-century travellers often carried with them a whole array of other documentation. A passport issued by the magistrate where you lived made it simpler to traverse the countless border crossings between the dozens of baronies, counties and principalities, and above all it granted you unrestricted access to the cities. Moreover, it was a means of preventing overzealous customs officials from turning your baggage inside out, even if bribery was often a far more efficient strategy. Tolls also had to be paid continually on roads and waterways. Albrecht Dürer, who travelled to the Netherlands in 1520–21, kept on having to pull out his toll docket. Furthermore, *fede di sanità* – bills of health – were practical documents to hold if you wanted to travel about freely in regions afflicted by the plague, while medical certificates allowed Protestant travellers to eat a portion of meat and drink a glass of wine during Lent. Letters of recommendation issued by renowned scholars were essential in gaining access to museums, libraries, cabinets of curiosities and numerous other collections.[17]

How – *a map of prime destinations*

When looking at a map of the prime destinations in the 16th century, it is Italy, France and Switzerland that had by far the highest profile, whereas England, the German principalities and the Netherlands paled by comparison, and regions such as the Iberian Peninsula, Eastern Europe and Scandinavia remained a complete blank. Anyone travelling to the latter areas generally did so out of necessity: diplomats on their way to the Spanish court, merchants in search of high-quality Swedish iron ore, or people seeking to recruit mercenaries in Poland. Moreover, such regions often lacked the infrastructure to receive travellers; inns there were particularly scarce, or else absent, compelling people to spend the night on a bed of straw or sleeping beneath the stars, while the transport infrastructure was often terribly basic. For example, Northern and Southern Netherlands travellers often experienced their journey through Spain as one of unbridled adventure in which on some routes in the mountainous interior they were confronted with highwaymen, mule caravans and impoverished *ventas* [inns], where there was no food or drink to be had. Sometimes Northerners would also get a culinary shock from the goat stews and other local specialities that could be bought at markets. What is more, the searing heat took a heavy toll on them as well.[18]

Such negative experiences were also the stuff of journeys to the other extreme of Europe. Even in the late 17th century, the Amsterdam merchant Abraham van der Meersch chose to describe his trip to Sweden as a brutal voyage of survival. Readers of his journal find themselves mercilessly carried off on the life-threatening crossing of a frozen sea of ice known as the Great Belt, as well as a dreadful sledge ride through the oppressive forests of Scandinavia and an improvised overnight stay in a lonely and dilapidated hut. Van der Meersch borrowed a part of his storyline from the immensely popular account told by Willem Barentsz and Jacob van Heemskerck about the terrible winter they spent on Nova Zembla.[19] This illustrates rather nicely that we sometimes need to take all these tall stories with a pinch of salt. After all, just as nowadays, travellers then felt the urge to richly embellish dangers and risks, thus emerging as the hero of the piece by stoically and steadfastly withstanding each perilous episode.[20] However, such inventories of tall stories spilled forth not only in the context of Northern, Southern or Eastern Europe, but also occurred in accounts of more conventional Grand Tours through France and Italy, when travellers passed through forested or mountainous terrain. In the late 17th century, Balthasar III Moretus – one of Plantin's descendants – had no hesitation at all in typecasting his short journey to Scherpenheuvel as a pocket-sized adventure, with his travelling party, on finding themselves in a regional forest, coming eye-to-eye with bears, wolves and other wild animals.[21]

In the late 16th and early 17th centuries, Italy remained the principal destination *par excellence* for hordes of pilgrims, merchants, students and Grand Tour travellers. On the outbound journey, many of them made a detour through France. That being the case, Paris was an important initial stop, although the city's still largely medieval appearance was not always to everyone's taste. Nevertheless, the metropolis had been given a new look thanks to a whole host of projects undertaken by Renaissance royalty, such as Francis I, Henry II and Henry IV, including the Louvre, Fontainebleau, the Place Royale and the Pont Neuf. After their stay in Paris, a great many travellers undertook a 'little tour' of France. This took them first of all past the Loire, where they strung together its Renaissance castles – Amboise, Blois and Richelieu. Very often they would also schedule a stay in one of the academies, where they took classes

10 Hendrick III Cleve (draughtsman); Philips Galle (publisher), *View of Rome*, 1551–1589.
Museum Plantin-Moretus, PK.OPB.0140.098

in fencing, dressage and other noble pursuits. Next, they would embark on a lengthy tour that took in Limoges, Bordeaux, Toulouse and Montpellier, ending up in Provence, where they could sample Classical Antiquity by admiring the Roman temples, amphitheatres, aqueducts, triumphal arches and other ancient remains in Nîmes, Arles and Orange. One classic *vaut-le-détour* was the Grande Chartreuse monastery that lay high up in the mountains of Savoy. Owing to its isolated location – accessible only via a narrow and steep mule path – it was yet another ideal spot for gazing in superlative style at towering cliffs of rock and plunging gorges. Grande Chartreuse was a warm-up for *les sept merveilles du Dauphiné* : a series of seven natural phenomena, including *le mont aiguille* [the unscalable mountain], *la fontaine ardente* [the burning spring], *les cuves de Sassenage* [natural basins in a cave] and other marvels.[22]

Savoy proved to be a fork in the road in many cases. Travellers would either cross from there over the Alps to Italy via the Mont Cenis Pass or else return back home via Lyon. The latter option increased in popularity in the late

16th century as the Reformation gained ever more ground and a journey to Italy became too fraught with risk for Lutherans, Calvinists and other Protestants. It was only in the early 17th century that the Inquisition began to adopt a more tolerant stance, leading to a considerable renewed influx of Dutch, German and English travellers. Naturally enough, no obstacles were placed in the way of Catholic travellers. Once over the mountains, Northerners would visit a long list of cities famed for their art – *Milano la grande*, *Genova la superba*, *Bologna la grassa* and *Ravenna l'antica* – with Venice, Florence, Naples and Rome standing head and shoulders above all of them. Curious visitors were drawn to an exceptional cocktail of stunning Renaissance art and relics from Classical Antiquity.

Nowhere did this symbiosis come into sharper focus than in Rome and, more particularly, in the Vatican, where visitors stared in awe at Michelangelo's frescoes in the Sistine Chapel or the Raphael Rooms, while at the same time being mesmerized by the classical sculptures such as the Laocoön Group. Given its classical landmarks, such as the Roman Forum, the Colosseum, the Pantheon, the Catacombs and innumerable other sites, the city offered a splendid sampling of Roman architecture, while visitors to the Farnese, Medici and Este collections were able to marvel at sculpture, cameos, mosaics and other 'finds'.[23] After such a cultural onslaught, the region around Naples had a very different kind of entertainment to offer. Here, typical Grand Tour travellers could witness all kinds of natural phenomena the Phlegraean Fields, where boiling hot geysers spurted from the ground; the Solfatara Crater, which was covered in a thick layer of sulphur, and, of course – the icing on the cake – the ascent of Mount Vesuvius, which sometimes spewed forth smoke and ash.[24] It was with such a cymbal clashing finale that most travellers rounded off their traditional *Grand Tour*. Time, then, for them to wend their way home again!

Selective bibliography

Frank-van Westrienen, A., *De Groote tour. Tekeningen van de educatiereis der Nederlanders in de zeventiende eeuw*. Amsterdam, 1983.

Mączak, A., *Travel in Early Modern Europe*. Oxford, 1995.

Verhoeven, G., *Europe within reach. Netherlandish travellers on the Grand Tour and beyond (1585-1750)*. Leiden, 2015.

It is also worth reading the accounts of journeys undertaken by Albrecht Dürer and Fynes Moryson at:

https://archive.org/details/albrechtdrersta00drgoog/page/n11

https://ia902605.us.archive.org/26/items/itinerarycontain04moryuoft/itinerarycontain04moryuoft.pdf

Endnotes

1. From *Divertissement*. Quoted in: D. Roche, *Humeurs vagabondes. De la circulation des hommes et de l'utilité des voyages*. Paris, 2003, p. 10.
2. Nowadays, there is a stronger emphasis on society's mobility: Roche, *Humeurs vagabondes*, pp. 10-15.
3. For more information about these pilgrims, see: M. Vaes, 'Les fondations hospitalières flamandes à Rome du XVe au XVIIIe siècle', *Bulletin van het Belgisch Historisch Instituut te Rome* 1, 1919, pp. 161–375; J. Van Herwaarden, *Between Saint James and Erasmus*. Leiden, 2003, pp. 136–42; R. Davis, 'Pilgrim-Tourism in Late Medieval Venin', in: P. Findlen *et al.* (ed.), *Beyond Florence. The Contours of Medieval and Early Modern Italy*. Stanford, 2003, pp. 119–32.
4. L. Voet, *The Golden Compasses: A History and Evaluation of the Printing and Publishing Activities of the Officina Plantiniana at Antwerp*. Amsterdam, 1969.
5. Roche, Humeurs vagabondes, pp. 972–80; L. Milis, 'Travellers of the Southern Low Countries and their views on Italy and the Italians', in: *Bulletin van het Belgisch Historisch Instituut te Rome* 61, 1991, pp. 7–35; H. Gräf & R. Pröve, *Wege ins Ungewisse. Reisen in der Frühen Neuzeit, 1500–1800*. Frankfurt, 1997, pp. 20–3; J. Heringa, *De eer en hoogheid van de staat. Over de plaats der Verenigde Nederlanden in het diplomatieke leven van de zeventiende eeuw*. Groningen, 1961, pp. 137–8.
6. To read more about this educational journey, see: G. Verhoeven, *Anders reizen? Evoluties in vroegmoderne reiservaringen van Hollandse en Brabantse elites*. Hilversum, 2009; A. Frank-van Westrienen, *De Groote Tour. Tekeningen van de educatiereis der Nederlanders in de zeventiende eeuw*. Amsterdam, 1983; H. De Ridder-Symoens, 'Mobility', in: H. De Ridder-Symoens (ed.), *A History of the University in Europe*. Cambridge, 1996, II: 416–48.
7. Among other material, read the correspondence concerning his sons in: the Nationaal Archief in The Hague, F. A. van Aerssen 6–8, F. van Aerssen, *Eigenhandige kopieën van brieven* (1607–08).
8. For more information on transport, see: A. Mączak, *Ontdekking van het reizen. Europa in de vroegmoderne tijd*. Hilversum, 1998, pp. 15–44; H. Scott, 'Travel and Communications', in: H. Scott (ed.), *The Oxford Handbook of Early Modern European History, 1350–1750: I – peoples and places*. Oxford, 2015, pp. 166–92; Frank-van Westrienen, *De Groote Tour*, pp. 88–118.
9. Quote from: Mączak, *Ontdekking*, p. 21.
10. To read further about these dangers – purported or otherwise – see: Mączak, *Ontdekking*, pp. 19–30.
11. For more information about the genre, see: G. Chabaud *et al.* (ed.), *Les guides imprimés du XVIe au XXe siècle. Villes, paysages, voyages*. Paris, 2000.
12. Quote from: Mączak, *Ontdekking*, 52.
13. J. Gallagher, *Learning Languages in Early Modern England*. Cambridge, 2019; Mączak, *Ontdekking*, p. 60.
14. University Library Leiden, Thys 151: S. de Bacher, *Reisbrieven aan zijn ouders* (1608–11).
15. For further information about homesickness and other emotions, see: S. Goldsmith, "Nostalgia, homesickness, and emotional formation on the eighteenth-century Grand Tour', *Cultural and Social History* 15 (2018), pp. 333–60.
16. Mączak, *Ontdekking*, pp. 107–36; Frank-van Westrienen, pp. 81–4.
17. A. Dürer, *Tagebuch der Reise in die Niederlande* (ed. F. Leitshuh). Leipzig, 1884, pp. 50–1.
18. Mączak, *Ontdekking*, pp. 70–2.
19. Verhoeven, *Anders reizen*, p. 26.
20. For further information about this pose, see: S. Goldsmith, 'Dogs, Servants, and Masculinities: Writing about Danger on the Grand Tour', *Journal for Eighteenth-Century Studies* 40, 2017, pp. 3–21.
21. Museum Plantin-Moretus, M 90² III-IV: B. III Moretus, *Reijse ghedaen door Balthasar Moretus den jonghen*. 1668.
22. M. Boyer, *Histoire de l'invention du tourisme, XVI-XIX siècles*. Paris, 2000, pp. 13-34; J. Stoye, *English Travellers Abroad (1604–1667)*. New Haven, 1989, pp. 35–43; Frank-van Westrienen, *De Groote Tour*, pp. 255–72.
23. W. Stenhouse, 'Visitors, Display and Reception in the Antiquity Collections of Late Renaissance Rome', *Renaissance Quarterly* 85 (2005), pp. 397-434;
24. Stoye, *English Travellers*, p. 134.

"Let a Traueller obserue the vnderwritten things, & of them some curiously, some slightly, as he shall iudge them fit for his purpose. He shall obserue the fruitfulnes of each Countrey, and the things wherewith it aboundeth, as the Mines of mettals and precious stones, the chiefe lawes and customes of the workers in those Mines, also Batches and the qualitie of the water, with the diseases for the curing whereof it is most proper, the names springs and courses of Riuers, the pleasant Fountaines, the aboundance or rarity of Pastures, Groues, Wood, Corne, and Fruits, the rare and precious Plants, the rare and proper Beasts, the prices of necessary things, and what he daily spends in his diet and horsemeat, and in hiring Horses or Coaches, the soyle of euery dayes iourney, the plenty of Fishes or Flesh, the kinds of meat or drinke, with the sauces and the rarer manners of dressing meates, the Countreys expence in apparell, with their constancy or ficklenesse in wearing it, the races of Horses, as the Giannets of Spaine, the Coursers of Naples, and the heauy Horses of Freesland, and how they manage and feed these Horses, the scituation of Cities and Prouinces, the healthfulnes of the Aire, the Chorography, the buildings, the ritches, the magnificence of Citizens, their houshold stuffe, and in generall all speciall things, as Statuaes, Colosses, Sepulchers with the inscriptions, Lybraries, with the most rare Bookes, Theaters, Arches, Bridges, Forts, Armories, Treasuries, Monasteries, Churches, publike houses, Vniuersities, with their Founders, reuenewes, and disputations. To conclude, let him visit the most learned men, and those that excell in military Art or any vertue, and let him conferre with them, as his ends require."

"The Traueller shall further obserue the policy of each State, and therein the Courts of each King or Prince, with the Courtiers entertainements, fees, or offices, the statures of the Princes, their reuenewes, the forme of the Commonwealth, whether the Prince be a Tyrant, or beloued of the people, what Forces he hath by Sea or Land, the military discipline, the manners of the people, their vices, vertues, industry in manuall Arts, the constitution of their bodies, the History of the Kingdome, and since the soule of each man is the man, and the soule of the Commonwealth is Religion, he shall obserue the disposition of the people, whether it be religious, superstitious, or prophane, and the opinions of Religion differing from his, and the most rare Ceremonies thereof. He shall also obserue the trafficke of Merchants, and therein the commodities which they carry out, and most want, the Hauens and roades for Ships, their skill in nauigation, and whether they vse subiects or strangers for their Marriners. Lastly, the value of the Coynes in each Countrey, and the seueral currant peeces, and whatsoeuer he shall thinke meet to adde hereunto."

Plantin, a publisher forever on the road

Dirk Imhof

Curator of Books and Archives, Museum Plantin-Moretus, Antwerp

01 Peter Paul Rubens, *Portrait of Christophe Plantin*, Museum Plantin-Moretus, V.IV.47.

Old prints depicting a printing shop sometimes also display the owner of the firm. In such cases, he is depicted as a wealthy individual, sumptuously clad, casting a satisfied gaze over his workers' labours while he himself is disengaged from any work.[1] That image of the supervisory, passive publisher may serve as an appealing illustration, but it does not wholly correspond to the hectic life led by a successful publisher, much less that as lived by Plantin. A more accurate depiction would have had Plantin surrounded by baggage, ready to depart on yet another journey for the sake of some matter or other to further his business. For booksellers in the 16th century, it was completely natural to be frequently on the road to visit potential suppliers and clients. Numerous entries in the journals kept at Plantin's bookselling business attest to a dealer who was buying books "estant present" at the shop premises in Antwerp. Only important dealers could afford to have personnel in their employment to undertake such journeys. Plantin, too, was travelling several times a year for a great part of his career, not only on account of his bookselling business, but also to organize all manner of private matters.

The preserved correspondence and accounts offer scant information concerning the precise course and organization of Plantin's journeys. The letters written to his family members when he was travelling have not survived. Consequently, there is hardly any information about the places where he stayed overnight or where he partook of meals. We know no more than that he went from one place to another by horse or coach. It is only rarely that we read something about the number of days he was on the road or the route that he took. Despite these limitations, it is still worthwhile examining Plantin's busy itinerary more closely in order to obtain an overview of the most important places to which he travelled and why it was necessary for him to go there. This makes it all the more comprehensible just how demanding the life of an ambitious publisher was, and how, nevertheless, Plantin doggedly faced all those challenges with such success.

The first years of Plantin's career (1555–65)

As regards Plantin's first years as a publisher, there is very little concrete information about his travels. Only a few accounting documents and a handful of letters remain preserved from that time. We do know from one of the few documents to have survived that he was in Paris in August of 1556, but there is no information about precisely what he was doing there.[2] Before he came to Antwerp in 1548 or 1549, he had spent some time in the French capital together with his wife and first daughter. Also resident there was Pierre Porret, Plantin's boyhood friend, who had settled in Paris as an apothecary, and Pierre Gassen, a wealthy trader in textiles with whom Plantin did business. Plantin's collaboration with Gassen began in 1556 and chiefly involved Plantin's purchase from small-scale suppliers in the Netherlands of worked textile items (such as ruffs and handkerchiefs) and their subsequent sale to Gassen.[3] It is thus not illogical that Plantin should have travelled regularly to Paris. In 1562 Plantin returned to Paris for a longer period, because he stood accused in Antwerp on account of a heretical pamphlet that his workmen had printed. Together with his wife and children he stayed with Pierre Porret until he was able to return to Antwerp at the end of 1563.

Pierre Porret and Pierre Gassen were both active in the "Family of Love", a spiritual group headed by Hendrik Niclaes, who was attempting to overcome the antagonism between Catholics and Protestants. Plantin's name appears a few times in a chronicle of the "Family". The anonymous author relates how Plantin had friendships in Paris with wealthy merchants. Among them was also a successful jeweller who had told Plantin and Porret that after his death he would be giving his possessions to Hendrik Niclaes. When he died and the casket of valuables was opened, a great deal appeared to be missing. Plantin and Porret denied that they had anything to do with the theft of the precious gems. Thereafter, Plantin embarked on a journey from Paris to Kampen (in the Dutch province of Overijssel), a distance in excess of 500 km, for the purpose of visiting Niclaes. Plantin told him about the gemstones and that a number of them had disappeared. When Niclaes asked him about the contents, Plantin ultimately admitted that he had taken three of the gemstones for himself, because the jeweller had had an outstanding debt to him.

02 Matthäus I Merian, *View of Paris in 1620*, in: Martin Zeiller, *Topographia Galliae, sive descriptio et delineatio famosissimorum locorum in potenstissimo regno Galliae*, Frankfurt, Caspar Merian, 1655–1661, engraving inserted after p. 26. Museum Plantin-Moretus, B 115 I.

Niclaes did not trust Plantin for an instant, but he let matters lie. Plantin returned to Paris via Antwerp: "A while thereafter, Plantin, in silence, journeyed to Antwerp, and so from Antwerp thence to Paris".[4]

In 1563, back in Antwerp, Plantin re-established his printing firm with the help of a few of the city's wealthy merchants. Paris remained an important sales market for Plantin's print shop, and for that reason he continued to travel regularly

to the French capital even then. At times he was accompanied by his right-hand man in the book trade, his future son-in-law Jan Moretus. To accomplish the journey to Paris that took place in the summer of 1565, Plantin had purchased a horse for 15 guilders and had hired one for Jan Moretus for 4 guilders and 4 stuivers. They set out on 8 July and arrived on 13 July. However, Plantin was sick until 4 August. On 6 August they left for Antwerp again, where they arrived five days later.[5] This gives us an idea of how long it took to cover the distance between Antwerp and Paris. However, the accounts do not reveal where they lodged *en route*.

Plantin considered his trade with Paris so important that he opened a shop of his own there in the following year (1566).[6] The management of that shop was placed in the hands of Pierre Porret and Plantin's shop assistant Gilles Beys, who left for Paris in January 1567.[7] Over the course of the next few years, Plantin dispatched thousands of copies of his editions to this shop. Between the years 1567 to 1569 alone, the combined price of the books sent to Paris amounted to 18,881 guilders, a sum to the value of several houses put together. Every so often Plantin's personal presence would be required. Fortunately, he was also able to rely on Jan Moretus to make the journey now and then.[8]

It was not always for business reasons that Plantin travelled to Paris. In June 1571 his third daughter, Catherine, married Jean Gassen, a nephew of his business associate Pierre Gassen. To celebrate the occasion, Plantin was also accompanied by his wife, Jeanne Rivière. We lack any precise information about how this journey was organized or the course it took.

A year later, in a letter to the Spanish theologian Benito Arias Montano, Plantin wrote a tangled tale about a subsequent journey to Paris. The Duke of Alba had summoned him to the camp of the Spanish army in the vicinity of Mons. He fell sick while waiting there. When the duke notified him that he could return home (although the meeting did not take place), Plantin chose to go to Valenciennes for bloodletting. This journey was not without its perils. Spanish soldiers were on the lookout for refugees from Mons and for rebels attempting to flee to France. Plantin succeeded in reaching Valenciennes, where he was given the care he needed and was able to recover. At the hospital, Plantin received a letter from Pierre Porret. He asked that Plantin consent to giving Madeleine Plantin's hand in marriage to Gilles Beys so that she could obtain French nationality, thus allowing her legally to inherit property in France (Madeleine was visiting her sister, Catherine, at the time).[9] It is possible that Plantin withheld information on a number of matters in his letter to Arias Montano. On the night of 23 August 1572, St. Bartholomew's Day, numerous assassinations of Huguenots took place in Paris. It is likely that Plantin would have wanted to go to Paris in person to safeguard his business affairs there.

During his stay in Paris, he also managed to secure a letter of safe conduct to assist his movements in France. Employing the requisite bluff, he wrote to Arias Montano that he might even be permitted to bring along firearms (a "*bombarda*"):

"When in Paris, and on account of the actions taken by my friends, I obtained from the French king a letter of safe conduct, such as they call it. As a consequence, I and my family entire may travel through all France at any time, bearing firearms, small-arms and long (which none is permitted, not even if they be of noble stock), and such that I may have my wares brought wheresoever I or my agent will".[10]

In 1575 he had to go to Paris yet again to fetch back his daughter, Catherine. In 1574, robbers had murdered her husband, Jean Gassen, while he was journeying on business in the Netherlands. In July or August 1575, Plantin and his wife went together to Paris to bring Catherine back to Antwerp once more.[11]

The Frankfurt Book Fair

In addition to his shop in Paris, Plantin had a second important location where he could market his books: the Frankfurt Book Fair. This fair, where all kinds of other luxury goods and artworks were also traded alongside books, was held twice a year: in spring during the three weeks before Easter and for three weeks in the autumn, starting on the Monday between 6 and 12 September. Frankfurt served as an ideal meeting point location for traders from Italy, France, the Holy Roman Empire and the Netherlands. Furthermore, there were good connecting routes by land and water, facilitating the easy movement of goods. For a great many traders, Frankfurt was also the preferred place in which to manage their financial affairs. Many loans and payments were planned to coincide with the two times in the year when the fair was held. Hailing from so many different countries, all these traders brought with them their own currencies, such that a great deal of money needed to be converted and, as a result, banking accounted for a significant amount of the activity that took place there.[12]

Plantin was in attendance at the fair even in his very first years of working as a printer. He dispatched to the fair numerous copies of his own editions and, equally, purchased at the fair other dealers' books that he could sell on in Antwerp. His Antwerp clients informed him about books of interest to them so that he could then seek them out at the fair. Moreover, major French dealers from both Paris and Lyon also relayed their orders to Plantin for significant procurements at the Frankfurt Fair. By this means, Plantin became an intermediary between dealers present in Frankfurt and booksellers from Lyon and Medina del Campo, the most important market for books in Spain.[13] Plantin did not trade solely in books at the fair; sometimes he would also send paintings, maps and diamonds on behalf of other traders. He, himself, would buy in paper and typographical items such as punches and matrices there. Several thousand guilders' worth of books were sent to each fair, all packed inside four to six barrels, each one weighing 700 to 900 pounds.[14] Although Plantin did also purchase large numbers of books from other publishers at the fair, his sales there realized notably large amounts of cash money, much needed by Plantin in order to finance his business in Antwerp.

With regard to the Frankfurt Fair, and as in the case of his shop in Paris, Plantin was also able to rely on Jan Moretus, who either accompanied him or went there alone. The barrels of books for dispatch to the fair were sent off well in advance and stored in a warehouse hired by Plantin. This shipment was made by water, via Mechelen or Dordrecht, to Cologne and then onwards from there via the Rhine to Mainz from whence it proceeded via the Main to Frankfurt. A few days prior to the start of the fair, Plantin and Jan Moretus would make their own journey to Frankfurt on horseback. That journey also provided a good opportunity to sort out all manner of matters along the way. For example, they were able to settle outstanding debts or other business with bookdealers in Namur, Liège or Cologne. Taken together, these trips to Frankfurt and the management of business affairs at the fair all took up several weeks.

However, the journey to Frankfurt was not without its dangers. First and foremost, there were itinerant bands of thieves and soldiers in search of booty. In 1568, Plantin's return journey from Frankfurt was extended by a few weeks because of having to make a detour to avoid armed groups. In 1586, gangs of robbers had made all the roads to Lier, Mechelen and Leuven unsafe. Plantin's agent Jan Dresseler had been on the road to Frankfurt when he fell into the hands of outlaws, despite the fact that he had departed in a group of other traders with considerations of safety in mind. He was released only after Plantin had paid ransom money for him.[15] Aside from robbers or soldiers, Antwerp's traders risked imprisonment because of the city of Antwerp's unpaid debts. In letters to Andreas Masius dated 22 October 1570 and 18 March 1571, Plantin wrote that he and his son-in-law no longer dared to visit Frankfurt again.[16] He had learned of traders from Antwerp having been taken prisoner on account of those municipal debts. Consequently, Plantin had quickly taken to his heels. The traders were still stuck in their predicament at the time of Plantin's writing, and he saw little appetite on the part of Antwerp's council to see them freed.

Leuven – Brussels – Liège

It is clear from the above that Plantin was frequently on the road from Antwerp to Paris or

03 Dispatch of the first three barrels of books to the fair in Frankfurt in the spring of 1579.
Museum Plantin-Moretus Arch. 962, Cahier de Francfort, Quadragesima 1579.

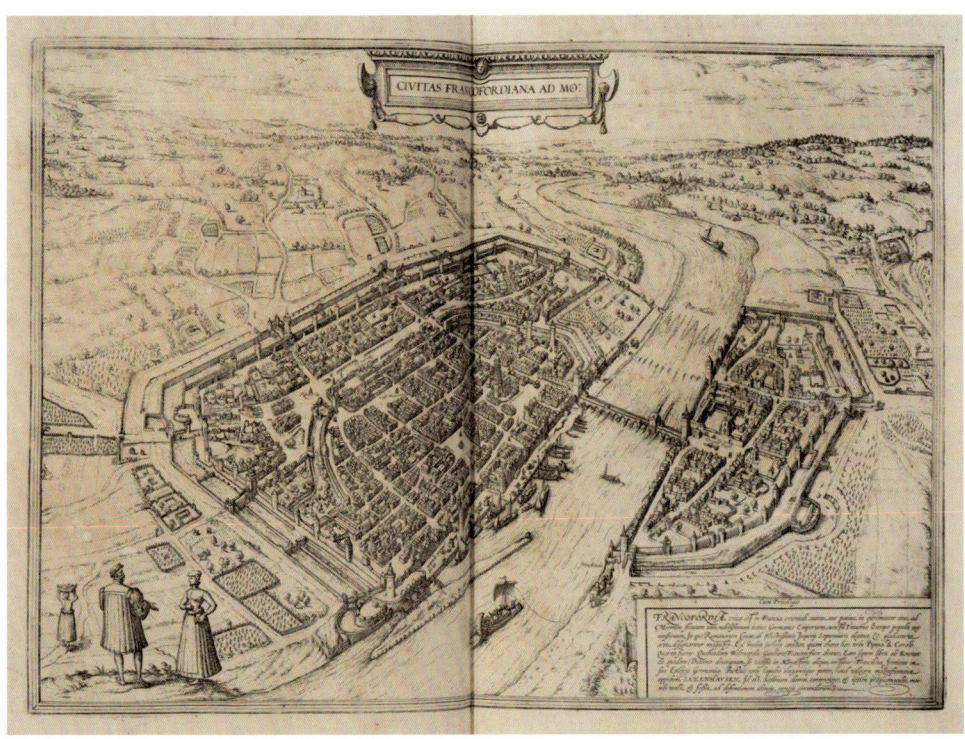

04 *View of Frankfurt, in: Urbium totius Germaniae Superioris illustriorum clariorumque tabulae antiquae & novae accuratissimé elaboratae*, Amsterdam, Joannes Janssonius, 1657, map 50. Museum Plantin-Moretus, B 49 I.

Frankfurt, but he also made regular shorter journeys within the Netherlands. What we would now consider short excursions, taking less than an hour's drive, were, in the 16th century, journeys that required travelling a day or more. In the 1560s, Plantin would often combine business in Leuven and Brussels. Leuven was where he regularly consulted with theologians from the city's university concerning editions of the Bible or to secure the approval required from them for one of his publications. He needed to be in Brussels to steer in the right direction applications for privileges from the Council of Brabant or Privy Council. In the 16th century, a publisher wishing to publish a work in the Netherlands firstly had to secure the assent of a religious censor, who had to verify that the text did not contravene Catholic doctrine (the *approbatio*). The publisher was then allowed to approach the Council of Brabant or Privy Council for a privilege that forbade other publishers from reprinting or selling the work for a certain period of time. This gave the authorities control over what could be published and gave the publisher exclusive rights over the sale of his work. Having personal contacts among the censors in Leuven and among council members and secretaries in Brussels could do much to further one's case.

In March 1564, Plantin embarked on a journey to Leuven and Brussels together with Isaac Levita, a professor of Hebrew from Cologne. Levita had already spent several months residing at Plantin's home for the purpose of working on a Hebrew grammar and dictionary. In thanks for their assistance in granting approval of these two works, Plantin recorded in his accounts that the priest of St. Peter's Church in Leuven (Cunerus Petri) and the Leuven theologian Augustinus Hunnaeus were each given a cheese from Auvergne and a basket of prunes, whereas Andreas Balenus, the Leuven professor of Hebrew, and a certain Master Adriaan were each in receipt of 2 guilders and 1 stuiver for their assistance. After Leuven, it was off to Brussels to request privileges for a few publications. The chancellor of the council was also given cheese and prunes as a gift. Plantin and Levita departed on a Sunday by coach and travelled via Mechelen to Leuven, where they spent the night. From Leuven they journeyed back and forth to Brussels and then from Leuven returned once more to Antwerp.[17]

In early September of the same year, Plantin was yet again in Leuven for a meeting with the city's theologians and with Andreas Balenus, this time for a review of the Hebrew Bible that Plantin wished to publish. The gifts were now copies of a few of his publications. Once again this involved a coach journey to Leuven, where he stayed for two days, and from there going back and forth to Brussels. From Leuven, the journey passed through Mechelen and back to Antwerp. He had to spend a further day and night in Mechelen to meet with Jacobus Susius in connection with the publication of Caesar's *Commentarii*. This sojourn had cost him an additional 18 stuivers.[18] Trips of this sort to Brussels and Leuven continued regularly over the course of the following years. In 1570 and 1571, he had to ride to Liège several times owing to a debt issue that remained unresolved.[19] Fortunately, his travels did include more pleasurable matters at times. On the evening of 3 May 1570 he was invited to dine with Thomas Gozaeus, a theologian from the University of Leuven who

05 Costs for the journey to Leuven and Brussels in March 1564. Museum Plantin-Moretus, Arch. 3, Journal des affaires 1563–1567, fol. 7v.

had proposed Plantin's publication of texts of the Church Fathers.[20]

The spring of 1568 proved an exceptionally busy time for Plantin. At the end of April, having only just returned from Frankfurt, he departed soon after for Brussels and Leuven. In Brussels he was summoned by the Duke of Alba's secretary to receive instructions concerning publication of the *Biblia Regia*, the multilingual edition of the Bible that Plantin had been allowed to print with the support of Philip II. Moreover, he obtained information about the arrival of Benito Arias Montano, a chaplain to the king of Spain, who was to oversee the printing of this royal Bible.[21] On 7 May 1568, Plantin wrote to Cardinal Granvelle that he would be departing in two days for France, where he would seek to purchase paper and parchment suitable for the *Biblia Regia*.[22] He had been in France for barely four or five days before he learned of Arias Montano's arrival in the Netherlands, requiring him to return back home from Paris via Brussels.[23] He was given little time to recover, because by June 1568 he was already travelling with Arias Montano to Leuven for consultations with the theologians there about the *Biblia Regia*.[24] In September, he took to the road for the Frankfurt Book Fair once again. On the return journey, at Arias Montano's request, he stopped in Kleef to visit Andreas Masius, an expert in Middle Eastern languages, to ask him whether he might use Masius's works in Chaldean and Syriac for the *Biblia Regia*. Thus, as his letter of 22 October 1568 to Cardinal Granvelle attests, this meant his return home was eighteen days later than usual.[25] It is hardly surprising that Plantin felt the work of the publishing firm was overwhelming him at times.

Travelling after the Spanish Fury

The years following completion of the *Biblia Regia* in 1572 proved Plantin's busiest with the production of thousands of liturgical works for Spain. This ceased thanks to the Spanish Fury suffered by Antwerp on 4 November 1576. Over several days, Spanish soldiers set out on a frenzy of looting and killing. It was only by paying off the soldiers that Plantin was able to see his printing firm spared. That sum of money, in total 2,867 guilders and 8 stuivers, was placed at his disposal by Luis Pérez, an Antwerp merchant of Spanish descent. In order to repay him and find the resources to cover repairs for the damage incurred, Plantin had to go in search of new loans, which once more meant long absences from home.[26] Plantin first travelled to Liège, where he sought help from Archdeacon Laevinus Torrentius (later, the Bishop of Antwerp).[27] He then departed for Paris, despite the winter weather and his poor state of health.[28] There, he arranged the sale of his Parisian shop, which ultimately came into the hands of the bookdealer Michel Sonnius for the sum of 7,500 guilders. From Paris, he travelled onwards to the Frankfurt Book Fair, where he met with his old associate Karel van Bomberghen, who loaned him 9,600 guilders. At last, after almost six months' absence, he arrived back in Antwerp in April 1577.

In the following year, Plantin set off for Paris for some three months. In a letter written in July 1578, he informed Arias Montano that, after the

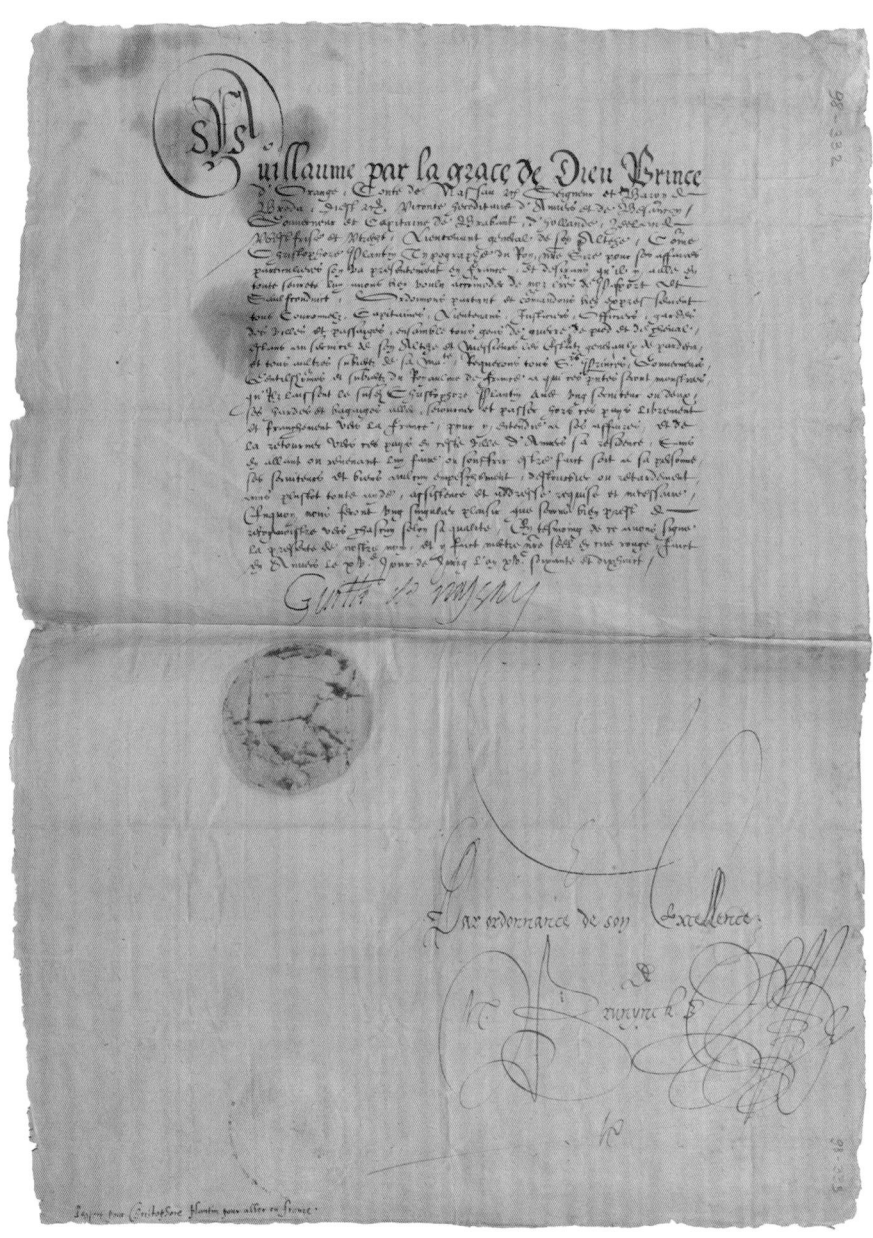

06 Letter of safe conduct allowing Plantin to travel to France.
Museum Plantin-Moretus, Arch. 98, Pièces de famille 1549–1589, p. 332.

marriage of his youngest daughter, Henriette, to Peter Moerentorf (the younger brother of Jan Moretus) he had placed the printing firm in the hands of his sons-in-law to give him time to pay visits to friends in Paris and various other cities in France.[29] The passport that he received for this journey from William of Orange, still survives. This provided him with a safe outbound journey for himself and one or two servants and, just as importantly, also a safe return journey to Antwerp.[30] A letter of safe conduct was an indispensable document for travellers at that time. Moreover, they also needed permission from their own city's authorities to embark on a journey abroad. To that end, Plantin had to swear an oath that he needed to travel to Frankfurt or Paris on business and would return immediately afterwards.[31]

The years 1580–85: travelling to the Northern Netherlands

Whereas in the years up until 1580 Plantin had travelled frequently to Paris and Frankfurt, in the years thereafter his focus turned chiefly to the Northern Netherlands. This coincided with the changing fortunes of war in the Netherlands in which the situation in Antwerp was becoming increasingly awkward. In the summer of 1581, Plantin had spent some time in Leiden and Utrecht. Each city attempted to persuade Plantin to set up his Press in their location.[32] Plantin settled on Leiden, where he arrived in November 1582 together with Raphelengius to buy a house which would enable him to start up a second printing firm in the spring of 1583. Once more, we know little about the way in which he moved about or precisely where he lodged. We know nothing at all about how and when his wife travelled to Leiden.

We are better informed about Plantin's return journey to Antwerp two years later thanks to a letter about it which he wrote to Arias Montano in early November 1585.[33] He decided to return to Antwerp in the summer of 1585. He travelled first to Amsterdam to board a ship bound for Hamburg "because it was not safe to take the shorter way overland owing to the brigands who are a threat to a journey by land". Despite a storm that, for several days, prevented the ship from sailing safely up the Elbe, ultimately they succeeded in mooring up at Hamburg. From there it was a journey by coach to Frankfurt, a distance of approximately 450 km that took several days to cover. Unusually, Plantin mentions in his letter the cities through which he passed *en route* (Lüneburg, Braunschweig, Kassel and Giessen, just to mention the larger ones). Having set off on a Tuesday, he arrived in Frankfurt on the Wednesday of the following week. There, he was met by Luis Pérez. He wrote that it was only then that he heard news of Antwerp's capitulation to the troops led by Alexander Farnese, the Duke of Parma. It was in a convoy of thirty coaches, and under the supervision of soldiers, that he made his return to Antwerp via Cologne, Liège (where he was received by Laevinus Torrentius) and Leuven (where he stopped to visit his theologian friends). He may well have felt by then that the time had come to consign all his travelling to the past. In the few remaining years of his life he appears not to have embarked on any more journeys.

In conclusion

Despite the lack of precise information about the way in which Plantin undertook his journeys, the roads he chose, where he lodged, and so forth, it is clear, nevertheless, that a great deal of his time was taken up in travelling through the Netherlands and to Paris and Frankfurt. It was in those last-mentioned cities that he would sometimes spend great lengths of time, on occasion voluntarily, at other times compelled to do so by outside forces. Consequently, if we were to paint an accurate portrait of Plantin, more likely than not it would have to be a portrait depicting him as a traveller on horseback or seated in a coach. For someone so frequently on the road, a peaceful day spent at home must have been all the more pleasurable, perhaps musing over a map from the atlas by his friend Abraham Ortelius, thus allowing him to examine the routes that dealers might be able to take, but this time without having to run any personal risk himself:

"Et si, sans te bouger, tu aimes mieux apprendre
Où le marchand s'en court chasque denrée prendre,
Icy tu le verras sans courir le danger
Des chemins perilleux, ni de la haute mer
Les flots impetueux."[34]

Endnotes

1. See, for example, the print "Impressio librorum" by Joannes Stradanus in the series *Nova reperta* or that on the title page of Hieronymus Hornschuch, *Orthotypographia*, Leipzig, Michael Lantzenberger, 1608.
2. Museum Plantin-Moretus, archive document no. 38, *Libraires et autres 1555–1562*, fol. 86 left. Further references to archival documents from the Museum Plantin-Moretus have been abbreviated below as "Arch.", followed by the number.
3. Concerning Pierre Porret, see Denis Pallier, "L'apothicaire Pierre Porret, ami et agent de Plantin", in: *De Gulden Passer*, 94:2 (2016), pp. 219–62; concerning Pierre Gassen, see Denis Pallier, "Recherches sur le cercle plantinien en France: amis, appuis, familistes", in *De Gulden Passer*, 96:1 (2018), pp. 11–21.
4. "Also overst, over ein tydt daer-nae, reisede Plantyn, dus in stilheit, to Andtwerpen, unde also van Antwerpen wedder to Parys", *Cronica. Ordo sacerdotis. Acta HN: three texts on the family of love*, ed. Alastair Hamilton, Leiden, 1988 (*Documenta anabaptistica Neerlandica*, 6; *Kerkhistorische bijdragen*, 15), chapter 21, 26, p. 72.
5. "Nous estions partis le 8 juillet 1565 et arrivasions a Paris le 13 de juillet et ay este malade audit lieu iusques au 4 aoust et partisons dudit lieu le 6 dudit mois dAoust pour nous en revenir et arrivasions en ceste ville dAnvers le 11 dudit mois dAoust la ou nous avons receu 4 tonneaux de marchandise …" (Arch. 3, *Journal des affaires 1563–1567*, fol. 32r).
6. Concerning this Plantin branch in Paris, see Henri Stein, "La succursale plantinienne de Paris", in: *Bibliographe moderne*, 1920–1921, pp. 34–57. Concerning the significance of Plantin's trade with France in general, see Malcolm Walsby, "Plantin and the French book market", in: *International Exchange in the Early Modern Book World*, eds. Matthew McLean and Sara Barker, Leiden, 2016 (*The Handpress World*, 38; *Library of the Written Word*, 51), pp. 80–101.
7. A payment for his travel expenses was noted on 7 January 1567 in Arch. 45, *Journal 1567*, fol. 62r.
8. Moretus was in Paris in July 1566 (Arch. 3, *Journal des affaires 1563–1567*, fol. 53v and 57r, and Arch. 36, *Journal 1561–1574*, fol. 109).
9. Plantin to Arias Montano, 1 November 1572; *Correspondance de Christophe Plantin*, eds. Max Rooses and Jan Denucé, 9 vols., Antwerp–Ghent, 1883–1920, no. 421, III, pp. 188–95. Further references to this publication of Plantin's letters have been abbreviated below as "Corr. Plantin". See also B. Arias Montano, *Correspondencia conservada en el Museo Plantin-Moretus de Amberes*, ed. Antonio Dávila Pérez, 2 vols., Madrid, 2002, no. 23, I, pp. 133–46.
10. Letter dated 1 November 1572; Corr. Plantin, no. 421.
11. Leon Voet, *The Golden Compasses. A History and Evaluation of the Printing and Publishing Activities of the Officina Plantiniana at Antwerp*, 2 vols., Amsterdam–London–New York, 1969–1972, I, p. 155.

12 Concerning the Frankfurt Fair in general, see John L. Flood, "'Omnium totius orbis emporiorum compendium': the Frankfurt Fair in the early modern period", in: *Fairs, Markets and the Itinerant Book Trade*, eds. Robin Myers, Michael Harris and Giles Mandelbrote, New Castle (Delaware)–London, 2007, pp. 1–42, and specifically regarding the fair's significance to Plantin: Karen L. Bowen, "The Antwerp Plantin Press and the distribution of images via Frankfurt in the 16th century", in: *Crossroads: Frankfurt am Main as Market for Northern Art 1500–1800*, eds. Miriam Hall Kirch, Birgit Ulrike Münch and Alison G. Stewart, Petersberg, 2019.

13 With regard to Plantin as the intermediary between Frankfurt and Salamanca in May 1566 for Charles Pesnot, see Arch. 3, *Journal des affaires 1563–1567*, fol. 50r. See also Dirk Imhof, "El comercio del libro de la imprenta-editorial de Plantino con Medina del Campo en siglo XVI y principios del siglo XVII", in: *El comercio del libro entre los Países Bajos y España durante los siglos XVI y XVII = De boekhandel met Spanje in het Europa van de 16de en 17de eeuw*, ed. Antonio Sanchez del Barrio, Valladolid, 2016, p. 34.

14 Karen L. Bowen, "The Antwerp Plantin Press and the distribution of images via Frankfurt in the 16th century", in: *Crossroads: Frankfurt am Main as Market for Northern Art 1500–1800*, eds. Miriam Hall Kirch, Birgit Ulrike Münch and Alison G. Stewart, Petersberg, 2019, pp. 67–8.

15 See Plantin's letter to Arias Montano dated 1 April 1586 (Corr. Plantin, VII, no. 1086 and B. Arias Montano, *Correspondencia conservada en el Museo Plantin-Moretus de Amberes*, ed. Antonio Dávila Pérez, 2 vols., Madrid, 2002, no. 93).

16 Corr. Plantin, III, nos. 364 and 368.

17 "Le 11 mars 1564 … Jay este a Louvain avec M. Jehan Isaac pour faire visiter sa grammaire en Hebrieu et le Thesaurus linguae sanctae Sanctes Pagnini a Brusselles pour solliciter le privilege de Virgile, Horace, Lucain et de tells vieux auteurs auquel voyage jay faict la despense qui sensuict estant parti le dimenche pour le chariot iusques a Malines patt. 10 en despense 3 patt. Pour le chariot de Malines a Louvain patt. 18. Jay faict present a Louvain au cure de St Pierre dun fromage dauvergne et 6 petits paniers de prunaux coustent le tout 2 – 3. A monsieur Augustinus Hunaeus docteur en theologie qui m'a adresse et recommande aussi 1 formage dauvergne et 6 paniers prunaux 2 – 3 … Pour depense de bouche audit Louvain et coucher(?) 3 – 6. Pour le chariot a Brusselles et revenir a Louvain – 17 … Despens audit Brusselles et retour de Louvain a Anvers 3 – 2" (Arch. 3, *Journal des affaires 1563–1567*, fol. 7v).

18 "Jay este a Louvain pour parler et solliciter ladvancement et proffict de limprimerie et ay paye a maistre Andre Balenus qui a visite la Bible en hebrieu 5 fl. 5 patt. et au cure 4 fl. 12 patt. … paye pour despense de chariot et 2 iournees de desp. 2 – 7 …Despense de chariot de de bouche 1 – 15. A Malines tarde un iour et 1 nuict pour attendre a parler a mons. Susius qui mavoit promis ses Comm. Caesaris et despendu tant en chariot que de bouche – 18. Pour le chariot a Anvers – 3" (Arch. 3, *Journal des affaires 1563–1567*, fol. 17r).

19 Corr. Plantin, II, no. 202: "Estant retourné de Liège, où j'avois esté appellé pour quelques affaires". Concerning this debt issue, see Denis Pallier, "Recherches sur le cercle plantinien en France: amis, appuis, familistes", in *De Gulden Passer*, 96:1 (2018), pp. 16–17.

20 Corr. Plantin, II, no. 226.
21 Corr. Plantin, I, no. 123.
22 Corr. Plantin, I, no. 125.
23 Corr. Plantin, I, no. 128.
24 Corr. Plantin, I, no. 133.
25 Corr. Plantin, II, no. 155.
26 Concerning this journey, see Leon Voet, *The Golden Compasses. A History and Evaluation of the Printing and Publishing Activities of the Officina Plantiniana at Antwerp*, 2 vols., Amsterdam–London–New York, 1969–1972, I, p. 87.

27 See Jan Moretus' letter to Arias Montano dated November 1576 (Corr. Plantin, V, no. 745).

28 See Jan Moretus' letter to Jean Moflin dated November 1576: "… mon beau pere lequel est allé faire ung voyage vers Liege et de la a Paris en ce temps d'yver lequel est tant contraire a (sa) santé comme le scavés, mais la nécessité l'a a ce contraint" (Corr. Plantin, V, no. 746).

29 Corr. Plantin, V, no. 801.

30 Arch. 98, *Pièces de famille 1549–1589*, p. 322. For a transcription of this document, see *Supplément à la correspondance de Christophe Plantin*, ed. M. Van Durme, Antwerp, 1955, no. 242, pp. 276–7.

31 With regard to such documents from the year 1568, kept at the Antwerp municipal archives (Felixarchief), see the transcriptions in *Supplément à la correspondance de Christophe Plantin*, ed. M. Van Durme, Antwerp, 1955, nos. 233–5, pp. 261–2.

32 With regard to Plantin's presence in Leiden in June–July 1581, see *Iusti Lipsi Epistolae*, pars I: 1564–1583, Brussels, 1978, pp. 28–286 and 290–1 (ILE 81 06 04 and 81 07 07); concerning Plantin's sojourn in Utrecht, see Maurits Sabbe, "J. Lipsius en Chr. Plantin te Utrecht in 1581", in: *De Gulden Passer*, 5 (1927), pp. 10–12.

33 Corr. Plantin, no. 1045.

34 Plantin to the reader, in Abraham Ortelius, *Le théatre du monde*, 1587.

"And because the memory is weake, and those who write much, are many times like the Clerkes that carry their learning in their Booke, not in their braine, let him constantly obserue this, that whatsoeuer he sees or heares, he apply it to his vse, and by discourse (though forced) make it his owne. [...] Let him write these notes each day, at morne and at euen in his Inne, within writing Tables carried about him, and after at leasure into a paper booke, that many yeers after he may looke ouer them at his pleasure."

❖

"Also I aduise him to leaue a trusty friend at home, who will keepe good credit with the Merchant that furnisheth him with money abroad, left his friends ill paiments leese him his credit, and so driue him to disgracefull wants. For if his friend pay readily, nothing shall be wanting to him."

❖

"For the danger or security of carrying money about him in all parts [...] In generall, he must bee warie not to shew any quantity of money about him, since Theeues haue their spies commonly in all Innes, to inquire after the condition of passengers. If his iourny be long, let him not tell (no not to his companions in his iourny) the furthest end thereof, but rather from Citie to Citie professe that he intends to goe no further. Suppose he bee at *Paris*, if he professe his iourny is from thence to *Rome*, it is all one as if he shewed his purse, since all men know, he must haue great store of money for that iourny, so as it were more fit he should professe onely to goe for *Strassburg* in *Germany*, or for *Lyons* in *France*, and when he shall come thither, he shall either perhaps haue new consorts of his iourny, or else may professe to his former consorts, that there he met with letters, which force him to goe further."

" [...] he shall doe well before he set forth, to get some skill (at least superficiall) in the Art of Cosmography, for if he be altogether ignorant thereof, he shal, like a blind folded man, not know where he is, or which foot first to set forward."

"For the Precepts before hee set forth, in the last place I aduise him to make his will, which no wise man staying at home will haue vnmade."

In Plantin's Footsteps

—

Cédric Raskin

Photographer

I could sense it at once from the brown smudge on his smart white shirt; the man sitting in front of me does not like travelling. The honking of car horns, the beeping of ticket barriers and the buzzing of sliding doors. Delays on the track, tailbacks on the road, bad Wi-Fi reception at the petrol station. And on top of that those blasted cardboard coffee cups. Too small, too flimsy, too expensive. And forever toppling over. Today, to cap it all, in the wrong direction.

Antwerp - Vrijdagmarkt

Travelling trophies ... you could collect a whole series of them. Coffee stains on freshly laundered cotton. A long curling hair left on your headrest. A half-smoked cigarette cast aside on the platform. Metro tickets littering the ground. A lichen-like encrustation of chewing gum, fag ends crushed underfoot between the brick paving, sausage-roll crumbs beneath the bench. A double set of trolley tracks emerging from a puddle of rainwater. A cloud of perfume from a tweedy passer-by. Each facet bearing silent witness to a popular phenomenon; this is where people are travelling.

Cart tracks in the mud

People travelled in the 16th century too. Not because they could, but rather because they had to. For example, if you had business to deal with abroad, just as in the case of Christophe Plantin. As well as attending to his print shop in the heart of Antwerp, the man also had to cross the border every so often. To Leiden, where he had a second branch of his firm. To his book shop in worldly Paris, and to his 'repository' in Frankfurt, for the book fair.

At that time travelling was a serious undertaking; the world then was utterly different from ours today. You didn't travel from country to country, but from city to city. From one inn to another, and from one principality to the next. Continually crossing new borders and coming face-to-face with different attitudes. It was a long, often dangerous, journey through fields, forests and swamps. You had to protect yourself against aggressive highwaymen, corrupt officials

Leiden - Vrouwensteeg

and devious innkeepers. And you had to ensure that every night, at each point along the way, there was safe lodging for horse, carriage and passengers alike.

Moreover, the journey had to be meticulously planned: plotting the safest route, preferably through peaceful and accessible terrain. You needed official letters of safe conduct for customs, convincing documentation to avoid difficulties, and, not least, a well-filled purse – albeit one that wasn't *too* visibly bulging with cash. A matter of not putting wrong ideas into the heads of unscrupulous passers-by *en route*.

Above all else, your journey would have proceeded slowly. Excruciatingly slowly. The horses' hooves would plod sluggishly along the pitted roads, as the fatigued draught animals lugged the heavy, juddering cart or carriage forwards. Great iron-clad wheels would leave behind deep tracks as they slushed through the mud. A slowed-down pace of life was then the norm, five centuries before that concept became aspirational.

Hot on Plantin's heels

Things are quite different now, of course. Wheeled luggage drives people in a hurry forwards. Mechanical escalators haul people upstairs and down again. Whether commuters, or day-trippers, they're all travellers. Latecomers race, their tickets clenched between teeth. A portly businessman strains to sprint, kids armed with bags of sweets weave about. I sit on a bench at the station and observe.

Until a French voice suddenly reverberates through the loudspeakers; my high-speed train is about to arrive at the Parisian station. This proves to be the starting signal for further commotion at the Gare du Nord. People spring straight out of their seats, magazines are stowed away, suitcases start rolling *en masse*, tickets are pulled from pockets. I, too, get myself in gear for my return journey to Antwerp. And then this journey will also be over. The last one of the three.

That's because over the past few weeks I've been travelling around on a special mission. With my camera at the ready and my eyes wide open, I set off in the footsteps of that intrepid business traveller. Just like Plantin, albeit five centuries afterwards, I travelled from Antwerp to the same three places: the narrow Vrouwensteeg in Leiden, the *Messe* in Frankfurt, and the busy Rue St. Jacques in the heart of Paris.

Paris - Rue St. Jacques

I saw things that Plantin could never have known, because in the space of five hundred years everything has changed. Horse and cart have been replaced by diesel and bodywork. Dirt roads and forest trails have been converted into motorways and railway lines. Sluggishly jolting through the peace of nature has been swapped for travelling at dazzling speed along buzzing lanes of commercial activity. Whereas each of Plantin's journeys was an adventurous undertaking, I was simply engaged in going back and forth.

Frankfurt - Messe

Comfort in plastic

Instead of a horse and cart, I opted for the car, the high-speed train, the metro and the tram. Very comfortable, predictable and, above all, unbelievably fast. I travelled at a speed that no 16th-century humanist could ever have imagined, and within a customized travelling infrastructure that they couldn't have even dared dream about.

Fast travel is so taken for granted nowadays that one barely stops to think about it. Progress in the form of tarmac to create ultrafast highways: bold lines cutting straight through a tamed natural landscape, lined with minimalist and uniform travel-oriented architecture in the form of motorway oases, self-service and embellished metro stations. Everything precisely organized to make my journey as fast, efficient and pleasant as possible. I can get to any place I want and can get away again just as easily. It's all done properly without going over the top. Comfortable, but not excessively so. And I can refuel on caffeine at a payment terminal, on petrol at the pump and essential rest amid comfort in plastic.

Whereas in the past Plantin was able to stray from the right path at every fork in the road, getting lost nowadays is an extinct concept. Demarcated arrows, lines and uniform international symbols serve to give travellers constant reassurance and confirmation. We even see the same buildings time and again, whether we're travelling in Belgium, the Netherlands, Germany or France. Whereas each business trip was a wholly new adventure for Plantin, my three trips seemed remarkably alike.

Travelling has never been so easy; nowadays, everything would seem possible. Except, perhaps, time travel. Can we still chase after the past today?

TO FRANKFURT: 396 km
TO PARIS: 348 km
TO LEIDEN: 147 km

Rösrath

Antwerp — Brussels — Paris

Fresnoy-lès-Roye

Antwerp · Paris

Hazeldonk

Antwerp — Leiden

Eschweiler

Antwerp　　　　　　　　　　　　　　　　　　　　　　　　　　　　　　　　　　Frankfurt

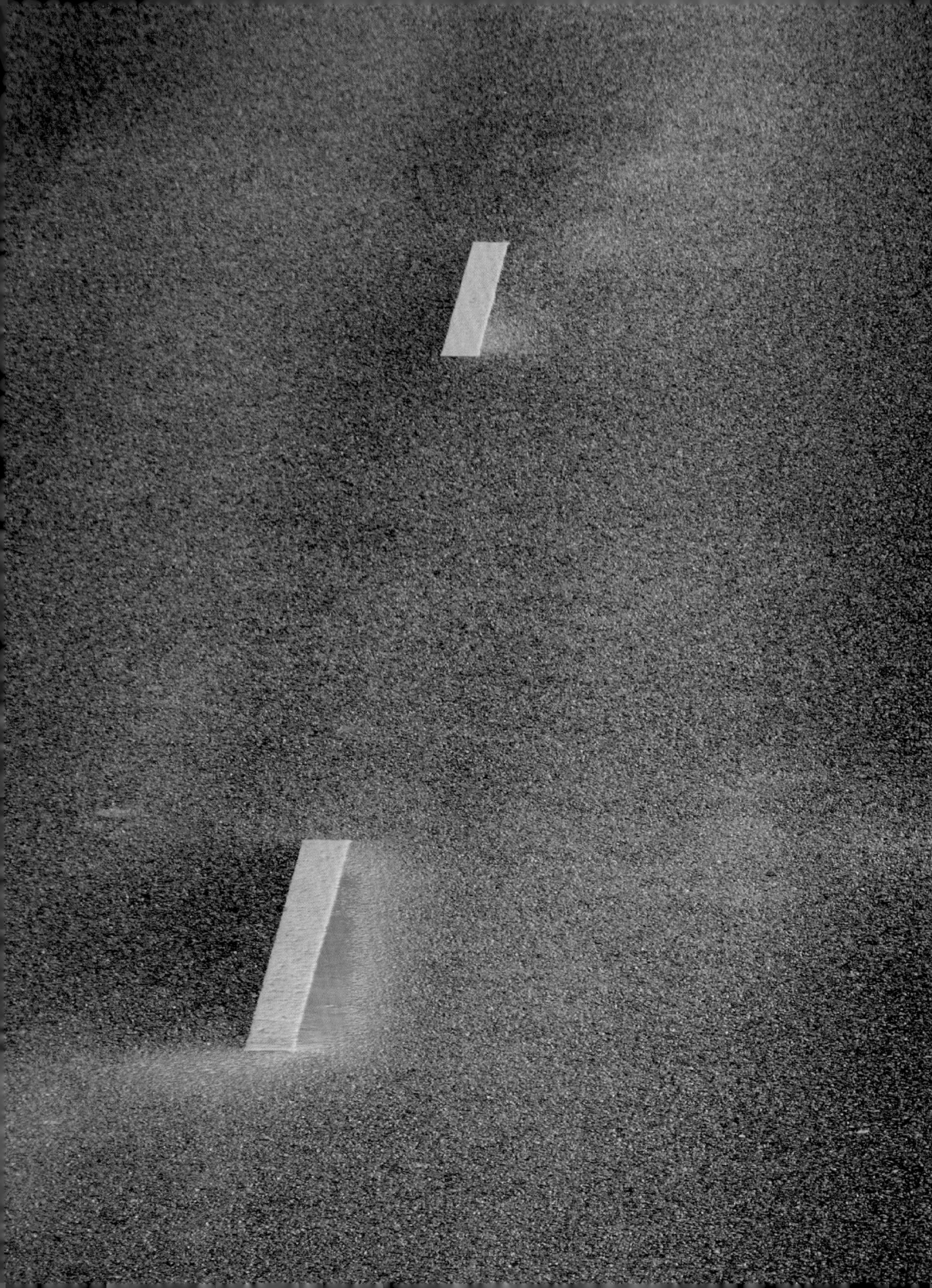

Bonn

Brussels

Heiligenroth

Antwerp   Frankfurt

Antwerp Leiden

Bocholtz

Antwerp

Frankfurt

Ranst

Antwerp — Frankfurt

Antwerp Leiden

Bonn

Heerlen

Minderhout

"When he hath once begun his iourney, since at the first step the ignorance of language doth most oppresse him, and hinder the fruite he should reape by his iourney, while he being as it were deafe and doumb, and astonished with this Babylonian confusion of tongues, can neither aske vnknowne things, nor vnderstand other mens speeches, by which hee might learne much. My aduice is, that in each Kingdome which he desires most to know, and the language whereof is of most vse in his owne Countrie, [...] where hauing learned the language, at least as much as is necessary to vnderstand, and to bee vnderstood, he shall make his next iourny more profitable by discourse, and in the same make his language more perfect."

"As it is good before his setting forth, to be reconciled with his enemies, that they may practice no ill against him or his friends in his absence, and that his mind may be more religiously composed against all euents; so while he is abroad, let him often write to his friends of his health [...] And this is no lesse good to himselfe, then to his friends, since he that writes often, shall often receiue letters for answere. [...] For indeed, there can hardly be giuen a more certain signe of loue or contempt, then thr (sic) frequent, rare, or no writing, or especially answering of Letters."

"When he wil obserue the scituation of any City, let him (if he may without ielousie of the Inhabitants,) first climbe one of the highest steeples, where hauing taken the generall scituation of the City, he shall better remember in order the particular things to be seene in the City. To which end, let him carry about him a Dyall, which may shew him the North, South, East, and West, which knowne, he shall lesse erre in the description of the City, and this he may obserue publikely onely with his eyes, for auoiding of ielousie, and after, being retired into his Inne, may draw it in paper, if he thinke good."

"Many desire to haue their Countreymen and friends to bee their companions in these their iourneys. [...] But why should he not rather desire consorts of the same Nation, of whom he may learne the language, and all other things worthy to be obserued. My selfe could neuer see any profitably spend their time abroade, who flocked together with their owne Countreymen, [...] since Trauellers meet with more dangers then pleasures, it is most fit for them to take such consorts abroad, as the way yeelds, and to deferre the imparting of their good successes to their friends, till their happy returne home, at which time, as their absence hath sharpened their friends desire to see them, so the discourse of these pleasant accidents, may sweeten their conuersation."

Mobility and Stability
Jost Amman's representation of trade, transport and travel in the early modern period

—

Christophe Schellekens
Research associate, Leibniz Institute of European History (IEG), Mainz

In 1585, the Swiss-German engraver Jost Amman designed the print *The Allegory of Commerce with a View of Antwerp*. The print shows us multiple scenes of commercial activity in the early modern period. It is no accident that Amman chose to represent these many scenes with Antwerp serving as the backdrop. After all, throughout the 16th century, this city had expanded to become the most important commercial centre in Europe. The various commercial activities displayed in the print were being conducted at a hectic pace. The goods depicted in the woodcut and named in its text found their way to Antwerp from across the whole of Europe and beyond, and from there were reshipped to other places. However, it was not goods alone that reached Antwerp, but also people – chiefly men – who were travelling to this trading hub within the context of their business endeavours. But just how did these journeys unfold? What were the principal routes and modes of transport? Which goods and people arrived at Antwerp? And just what was it about Antwerp that made it so attractive? In this essay, we shall explore the world of 16th-century trade, with Amman's depiction of commercial activities serving as our guide. The role played by Antwerp and the importance of mobility will be the common thread running through this.

Business missions and Antwerp's economic boom

The commercial success of Antwerp in the 16th century is inextricably linked to shifts in the mobility of people and goods during the first decades of that century. The commercial upswing of the High and Late Middle Ages caused people from a variety of European regions to seek their fortune through the ever risk-prone business of long-distance trade. The intensification of commerce led to important developments in the spheres of technology, practices, rules and institutions that served to keep the wheels of business turning smoothly. This also facilitated the rise of centres that were meeting points for traders and exchange locations for goods. In the Late Middle Ages, the focus of international trade shifted from the Champagne markets in France to the Flemish city of Bruges.[1] It was there that Venetian, Genoese, Lucchese

01 Jost Amman (engraver), *Allegory of Commerce with a View of Antwerp*, 1585.
Museum Plantin-Moretus, PK.OP.20701.

and Florentine merchants from Italy met with traders from the German Hanseatic cities and from France, Spain and other regions.

At the end of the 15th century, the position held by Bruges as the principal centre of commerce began to wane. It became increasingly difficult for shipping to access the city, owing in part to ever poorer navigability of the waterway between Bruges and the North Sea, but, above all, because the conflict with the Holy Roman Emperor, Maximilian I, made the city less and less attractive to international merchants. Antwerp was an appealing alternative. However, this shift from Bruges to Antwerp as the most important commercial centre took place gradually.[2] Even during the 15th century Antwerp had already become an important market place. Throughout that century, the Brabantian trade fairs in Antwerp and Bergen op Zoom exerted a pull on merchants based in Bruges. They completed financial transactions there and traded with English merchants

02 Basin with Latin descriptions for a variety of goods. On the base of the pillar at the centre a reference is made to the importance of circumstances ("circumstantiae") in relation to trade.

who tendered their wool at the port. As a centre in which to market their key wares, the latter merchants had preferred Brabantian Antwerp above Flemish Bruges since the Late Middle Ages.³

According to conventional wisdom, besides the English merchants who offered their wool ("Lanae et vellera" on the basin at the centre of Amman's allegory), Portuguese and southern German merchants were also responsible for turning Antwerp into a leading trading city.⁴ Owing to their expeditions in the Atlantic and Indian Oceans, Portuguese merchants acquired far greater direct access to Europe's supply of spices. Consequently, spices ("Aromata") enjoy a prominent place in the list of goods placed by Amman on the basin at the centre of *The Allegory*. Portuguese merchants had to pay for these goods using metals such as copper and silver. The mining and processing of these metals was controlled to a significant degree by southern German merchants who owned mines throughout Central Europe. Looking at Amman's *Allegory of Commerce*, we can see a scene in the centre-left section where mining is depicted as an important part of the trading system. 'Metalla' is another of the entries in his list of goods. The needs and goods of these two groups were brought together in Antwerp at the beginning of the 16th century, when the first Portuguese ship laden with spices put into the port. A few years later, the king of Portugal set up a central point of sale for the bulk distribution of these exclusive products.

Alongside the English, Portuguese and southern Germans (traditionally seen as the key drivers in the rise of Antwerp with their respective trading in wool, spices and metals), there were also many other merchants travelling to Antwerp in the hope of making their fortunes from international trade. French and Spanish traders set up in business in

03 A convoy of carts is laden with goods. Some of these commodities have been furnished with unique identification marks.

Antwerp together with many Italians.⁵ The northern and central Italian commercial centres of Genoa, Lucca and Florence were particularly well represented in terms of trading in Antwerp.⁶ They traded in a multitude of products, with an emphasis on exclusive types of textile such as silk and high-quality, wool-based fabrics ("Panni et serica" in Amman's list). Although Antwerp's growth was originally explained chiefly on the basis of the interests of these foreign merchants, it has been demonstrated more recently that traders hailing from the Southern Netherlands – Antwerp's hinterland – also played an important role in the Antwerp market. They traded in local products from the region but were also a prominent force in trade with Venice.⁷

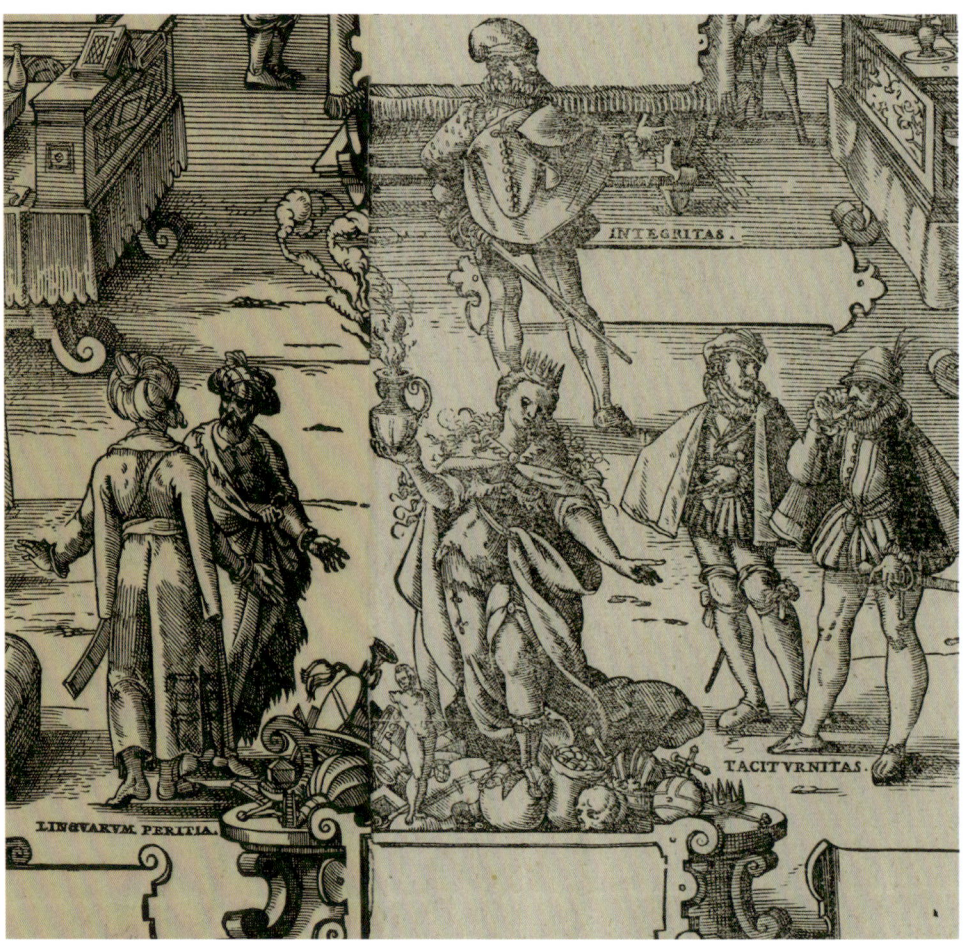

04 Merchants needed to possess numerous qualities: knowledge of foreign languages, integrity and understanding when to keep a tactful silence.

During the period of Antwerp's "Golden Age" – roughly the period between 1500 and 1585 – the city was thus an important meeting place for merchants from throughout Europe.[8] As far as we know, some of them, such as the French merchants, travelled regularly between Antwerp and their places of origin. Very often, traders from northern and central Germany also followed this pattern. There is less evidence of such lengthy journeys at regular intervals vis-à-vis merchants from southern Europe. Moreover, the need and willingness of merchants to travel great distances and establish themselves in a city far from their own city of origin was also dependent on a host of factors that evolved before, during and after the 16th century. Let us now delve more deeply into these challenges posed by international trade.

The organization, problems and dangers of international commercial travel

Since the second half of the 20th century, the citizens of Europe, including many business people among them, have found it increasingly easy and ever faster to travel long distances across the continent. The car, high-speed trains and aircraft have had an enormous influence on this. Moreover, the need to make payment in differing foreign currencies has also fallen by the wayside in recent decades, and national borders within Europe can be crossed without customs controls. If we are to grasp how journeys undertaken for the purpose of trade were accomplished, we need to put from our minds all of these modern-day circumstances and take ourselves back to a world in which international travellers had to overcome many more hurdles. First and foremost, the speed of travel was limited to the maximum capacity of wind power and that of physical human and animal power. Indeed, *The Allegory of Commerce* shows us several depictions of traders' horse-drawn carts in convoy. Weather conditions, seasons and terrain all played an important part in determining the rhythm and tempo of trade. What is more, Europe was a highly fragmented patchwork of many different states and sub-regions – large and small – with a multitude of legal and monetary regimes. This meant that travellers had to comply with many different obligations, and the transport of goods could be subject to all manner of toll regimes.[9] Some authorities chose to draft legislation that made it highly attractive to establish businesses in their city or state, whereas others imposed legislation that offered poorer prospects in a bid to protect their own merchants.[10] The reference to freedom ("libertas") in Amman's allegory refers implicitly to such possible restrictions and celebrates a freer type of policy.

Merchants also developed techniques, brokered deals, or founded associations in order to face the challenges posed by international trade. Via personal contacts in centres of commerce, they were able to conduct business with merchants from across Europe without always having to move about over long distances to enjoy an active presence in all those places. In the lower third of his allegory, Amman shows scenes that include such contacts. Merchants needed to possess the right qualities to operate successfully in this international environment.

The Allegory lists a number of these virtues. For example, a trader needed to have a command of foreign languages ("linguarum peritia"). To a great extent the languages spoken among traders of different origins remain guesswork, but written records give the impression that Antwerp in the 16th century was a multilingual environment. Documents were drafted in Dutch, French, Spanish, Italian and, occasionally, in Latin.[11] Italian merchants kept their books in Italian and likewise their correspondence, including that directed to recipients in the Netherlands.

In addition to linguistic competence, Amman also refers to a trader's other virtues and skills: fulfilling obligations ("obligatio"), maintaining a tactful silence with regard to confidential information ("taciturnitas") and acting with integrity ("integritas"). Such virtues aside, a trader's reputation also depended greatly on his personal reputation and that of his community. Since the Middle Ages, foreign merchants had often joined forces in commercial centres to form corporations or consulates.[12] These institutions represented the interests, the safety, and the good and solid reputation of a specific group of merchants. Their precise organization and composition varied a good deal according to the group of merchants and the city concerned. Some groups, such as the southern German merchants in Antwerp, were no more than a very loose coalition. Others, such as the English merchants trading in wool, formed a rigid organization that mounted boycotts and enforced internal discipline when faced with problems or disputes.

Alongside these traders' associations, the authorities in trading cities such as Antwerp also supplied services and infrastructure to facilitate the smoother operation of traders' businesses. Commercial interests were an important principle guiding the policy of Antwerp's mayor and aldermen.[13] In 1531, Antwerp's city council opened a new commodity exchange to provide the increasingly numerous merchants with an appropriate space in which to come together. The city also set up an official weighhouse, where merchants could have the official weight of their goods ascertained, as depicted by Amman in the lower left of *The Allegory*.

In addition to physical infrastructure, the city council also provided services to the mercantile community. Where necessary, rulings needed to be given swiftly, fairly and authoritatively in terms of reaching a judgment on disputes between traders. City clerks were made available to record business transactions and agreements in official documents, just as civil-law notaries would have done. Some of the certificates – documents registered by Antwerp's city clerks – offer a glimpse into the challenges faced by merchants in the course of their international traffic. In order to possess proof in the event of any disputes about ownership, or in the event of a loss or theft, merchants often drew up a declaration concerning the goods they intended to transport. Such documents usually entailed a description of the various goods to be carried via any form of transport, as well as the name of the dispatcher, carrier and recipient of the said goods. Moreover, the crates or barrels in which goods were transported were given a

05 Two merchants with a quantity of coins.

number and a distinctive identification mark. Amman shows us several examples of such marked goods in transit. These marks were also incorporated in the margins of certification documents so that, in the event of a disagreement, supporting documents would be available showing specific and precise details about the lost, stolen or disputed wares.

The problems that could be associated with transporting goods occurred under all kinds of circumstances ("circumstantiae" on the base of the pillar at the centre of *The Allegory*) and were legion. For example, a certificate dated 1547, documents the problems encountered by a certain Edward Henriques and Tomasso de Berti.[14] Henriques had had a consignment of fabrics and various other goods shipped

06 The balance between creditors ("creditor") and debtors ("debitor"). Merchants monitored this balance by keeping their letter-books ("Epistolar") and their accounts ("Zornal" and "Recor") up-to-date.

from Antwerp to the Italian port of Ancona. To that end, he had employed the services of the carrier de Berti. However, Henriques' goods had been seized in the territory of the Duchy of Mantua in northern Italy, because it was suspected that de Berti was a "Marrano Jew". The mercantile activities and presence of Jewish traders were subject to discriminatory restrictions and arbitrary prosecution in many parts of Europe. In 1542, most likely the same de Berti, but this time named in the document as Thomas Berti, had it officially recorded that he had had two crates of gold thread shipped from Florence to Antwerp for the business headed by the renowned Florentine Antinori family.[15] However, owing to war in France, this transport was held up and it had taken Berti a great deal more time to get the two crates to Antwerp. Amman was also aware that war and robbery were among the risks associated with international transport. In different parts of his allegory we see how soldiers are detaining a transport and, to the centre left, how they have set a farmhouse alight. Evidently, the roads along which mercantile traffic passed were subject to numerous dangers.

Alongside certificates and notarial deeds, the traders' own documentation also furnished them with an important means of overseeing their mercantile traffic, keeping track of their obligations and prospects, and getting an idea of their debts in relation to others and others' debts in relation to them. Long before the 16th century, debtors and creditors ("debitor" and "creditor" to either side of the weighing scales at the centre of *The Allegory*) were an important part of international trade. Financial traffic did not only concern the form of exchanging cash sums in the shape of coinage, as displayed by Amman. The fact is that even since the Middle Ages the bill of exchange had been an important alternative to the risk-laden transport of coin and precious metals over great distances.[16] In this document a debtor indicated that the sum owed by him to a specified person could be collected by an equally specified person in another, often far distant, city and in a particular currency. It was essential to this complex system of international financial transactions that merchants always kept proper track of their own debt position and kept each other up-to-date via correspondence. Their letter-books ("Ep[is]t[o]lar" in *The Allegory*), as well as the different aspects of their accounts ("Zornal" and "Recor"), were important instruments in that regard. If they were kept properly up-to-date, these documents also had significant legal value in court cases. Consequently, the letter writing and meticulous keeping of the accounts was an important component of a young merchant's education.[17]

Trading routes: by land or by sea?

As Amman's *Allegory* demonstrates, international trade involved both a personal component that unfolded in commercial centres such as Antwerp, as well as a part organized on paper through an exchange of letters and agreements. Naturally enough, both this correspondence and the confluence of goods and people from different corners of Europe and beyond could take place only as the result of couriers, carriers and traders travelling a variety of routes. However, which modes of transport were available to these travellers? Which routes led to Antwerp, and what motivated merchants to choose the specific route in question?

Amman's *Allegory* shows both the crowded shipping lane of the River Scheldt and also roads, where carts and travellers on horseback are seeking their way to and from the city. Antwerp was indeed as easily accessible by the road network as it was by water. It hardly needs stating that the choice of whether to go by road or navigable waterway was dictated in large part by the place from which a traveller set off on his way to Antwerp. A southern German merchant had no other choice than to travel for the most part by road to Antwerp, even if for sections of his journey he could use inland vessels that plied rivers such as the Rhine and the Main. By contrast, English merchants wanting to travel from Antwerp back to London needed to spend a good part of their journey aboard a ship in order to cross the English Channel. However, there were also situations in which one might opt to travel by road *or* by sea; in such cases merchants had to make a considered choice. Merchants from France, the Iberian Peninsula and Italy had various options before them when arranging their journey. Factors determining a decision to travel by land or sea were speed, cost and safety.

Two key considerations came into play when deciding whether to embark on a ship or to take to the road.[18] The cost of transport in relation to the price of the goods being transported was an initial significant factor. A second factor concerned safety and the risk of losing consignments. Convention has it that transport by a sea-going vessel is cheaper, because a larger volume of goods can be carried on one voyage. Therefore, relatively inexpensive goods transported in bulk could be carried more easily and cheaply by ship. There were two important risks that arose in respect of transport by ship: the risk of shipwreck and that of piracy. To deal with these risks, merchants developed ever more sophisticated insurance techniques over the course of the 16th century.[19] Nevertheless, transport by road remained an important alternative. After all, the higher cost of this mode of transport was a less important factor when it came to expensive luxury products.

The example of commercial traffic and merchants travelling between the Italian peninsula and the Netherlands demonstrates clearly how the preference for either a land route or a sea route could be subject to change. With regard to the commercial development of Italy, shipping traffic from the maritime republics of Genoa, Venice and, to a lesser extent, Pisa, had been an important historical factor in their success. Above all, it was the arrival in the 13th century of Genoese galleys in Bruges that caught people's attention. The situation was quite different in the 16th century. Genoa and Venice restricted the routes sailed by their galleys almost exclusively to the Mediterranean. Thanks to some unique toll-book records (1542–45), we know that Italian merchants transporting goods to and from the Netherlands did so largely by road.[20]

From the 16th century onwards, merchants were able to employ the services of specialist carriers. These professionals took responsibility for the numerous disparate elements involved in transporting goods, from the start to finish of the process. Whether customs duties, mandatory apportionment, or the use of the most appropriate means of transport according to the road infrastructure, these professional carriers complied with and organized it all. Alongside a few smaller players, such as the aforementioned Tomasso de Berti, transport between Antwerp and Italy was chiefly under the control of a handful of bigger players who came from the Italian and German-speaking regions around the Alps. Moreover, these carriers often focused on one specific route. One route of primary importance ran from Antwerp to Basel and thence across the Gotthard Pass to Milan or farther still into the Po Valley. The section between Antwerp and Basel followed the route passing through Luxembourg and Lorraine, or else via Cologne and the Rhine. In northern Italy, Italian carriers took charge of any shipments to further cities in central or southern Italy. A second important route ran from Antwerp to southern Germany, passing by the cities of Nuremburg or Augsburg and then passing through western Austria, ending up close to Venice. In addition to these two prominent transport routes, we know there was also a frequently used route running through France, which was employed by groups of merchants to travel from Italy to Antwerp or vice versa. For example, the Lucchese merchant Gherardo Burlamacchi recalled in his memoirs how, as a young lad of 14 in the summer of 1534, he had travelled for the first time to Antwerp on horseback and in the company of his brother and his wife. From Lucca their journey took them first to Lyon in France. This city was an important centre for the silk trade and banking matters, and played host to many Lucchese and Florentine merchants. In Lyon, Gherardo and his brother visited commercial partners and staff before continuing northwards on their journey. On average it would take such a company 30 to 40 days to travel from Lucca to Antwerp.[21]

07 Merchants were expected to be meticulous in attending to their correspondence and bookkeeping.

Conclusion

The world of international trade as described above also determined the ups and downs, successes or otherwise, of enterprises such as the Plantin Press. This business and many others owed their prosperity to the comings and goings of goods and people to Antwerp. At the end of the 16th century, 'Fortuna' turned against the commercial success of the city. The Dutch Revolt turned the region into a much less suitable meeting point for international merchants. In the early 17th century, the focus of commercial traffic turned to Amsterdam. Although the downturn was not comprehensive, and some important trading houses remained active in the city, Antwerp had nevertheless lost its role as the most important commercial centre in the region.[22]

Bibliography

Baetens, Roland, *De nazomer van Antwerpens welvaart : de diaspora en het handelshuis De Groote tijdens de eerste helft der 17de eeuw*, Brussels, 1976.

Brulez, Wilfrid, 'L'Exportation des Pays-Bas vers l'Italie par voie de terre, au milieu du XVIe siècle', *Annales. Économies, Sociétés, Civilisations* 14, 1959, pp. 461–91.

Coornaert, Emile, *Les Français et le commerce international à Anvers (fin du XVe-XVIe siècle)*, Paris, 1961.

De Smedt, Oskar, *De Engelse natie te Antwerpen in de 16e eeuw: (1496–1582)*, Mechelen, 1950.

Fagel, R. P., *De Hispano-Vlaamse wereld: de contacten tussen Spanjaarden en Nederlanders, 1496–1555*, Brussels, 1996.

Gelderblom, Oscar, *Cities of Commerce: the Institutional Foundations of International Trade in the Low Countries, 1250–1650*, Princeton, 2013.

Goris, Jan-Albert, *Étude sur les colonies marchandes méridionales (portugais, espagnols, italiens) à Anvers de 1488 à 1567 : contribution à l'histoire des débuts du capitalisme moderne*, Leuven, 1925.

Harreld, Donald J., *High Germans in The Low Countries: German Merchants and Commerce in Golden Age Antwerp*, Leiden–Boston, 2004.

Munro, John H., 'The Low Countries' Export Trade in Textiles with the Mediterranean Basin, 1200–1600: A Cost-Benefit Analysis of Comparative Advantages in Overland and Maritime Trade Routes', *International Journal of Maritime History* 11, 1999, pp. 1–30.

Pohl, Hans, *Die Portugiesen in Antwerpen: 1567–1648*, Wiesbaden, 1977.

Puttevils, Jeroen, *Merchants and Trading in the Sixteenth Century: the Golden Age of Antwerp*, London, 2015.

Schellekens, Christophe, *Merchants and Their Hometown : Florentines in Antwerp and the Duchy of Florence (c. 1500–1585)*, (doctoral thesis, European University Institute, Florence, 2018).

Van der Stock, Jan (ed.), *Antwerp, Story of a Metropolis:16th–17th century* (Antwerp, Hessenhuis 25 June–10 October 1993), Ghent, 1993.

Van der Wee, Herman, *The Growth of the Antwerp Market and the European Economy : (fourteenth - sixteenth centuries)*, The Hague, 1963.

Endnotes

1. J. Dumolyn & A. Brown, *Brugge: een middeleeuwse metropool, 850–1550*, Gorredijk, 2019.
2. J. L. Bolton & F. Guidi Bruscoli, 'When did Antwerp replace Bruges as the commercial and financial centre of north-western Europe? The evidence of the Borromei ledger for 1438', *Economic History Review* 61, 2008, pp. 360–79.
3. O. De Smedt, *De Engelse natie te Antwerpen in de 16de eeuw: (1496–1582)*, Mechelen, 1950.
4. The emphasis on English, southern German and Portuguese traders as the vehicles for Antwerp's growth can be traced back to Lodovico Guicciardini's description of the Netherlands: M. Limberger, '"Zo Schoon ende Bequaem tot versamelinghe der Cooplieden" [So fair and meet a place for the congregation of merchants] Lodovico Guicciardini's *Descrittione di tutti i Paesi Bassi* als bron voor de economische geschiedenis van Antwerpen', *Historiant. Jaarboek voor Antwerpse geschiedenis* 2, 2014, pp. 59–79. Jan. A. Goris, *Étude sur les colonies marchandes méridionales (portugais, espagnols, italiens) à Anvers de 1488 à 1567 : contribution à l'histoire des débuts du capitalisme moderne*, Leuven, 1925; H. Pohl, *Die Portugiesen in Antwerpen: 1567–1648*, Wiesbaden, 1977; D. J. Harreld, *High Germans in The Low Countries: German Merchants and Commerce in Golden Age Antwerp*, Leiden–Boston, 2004.
5. E. Coornaert, *Les Français et le commerce international à Anvers (fin du XVe-XVIe siècle)*, Paris, 1961; R. P. Fagel, *De Hispano-Vlaamse wereld: de contacten tussen Spanjaarden en Nederlanders, 1496–1555*, Brussels, 1996.
6. Goris, *Étude sur les colonies*; C. Beck, 'Éléments sociaux et économiques de la vie des marchands génois à Anvers entre 1528 et 1555', *Revue du Nord* 64, 1982, pp. 759–84; C. Beck, *La nation genoise à Anvers de 1528 à 1555 : étude économique et sociale* (doctoral thesis, European University Institute, Florence, 1982); R. Sabbatini, "Cercar esca": *Mercanti lucchesi ad Anversa nel Cinquecento*, Firenze, 1985; C. Schellekens, *Merchants and Their Hometown: Florentines in Antwerp and the Duchy of Florence (c. 1500–1585)* (doctoral thesis, European University Institute, Florence, 2018).
7. J. Puttevils, *Merchants and Trading in the Sixteenth Century: the Golden Age of Antwerp*, London, 2015.
8. H. Van der Wee, *The Growth of the Antwerp Market and the European Economy : (fourteenth-sixteenth centuries)*, The Hague, 1963; P. O'Brien et al. (ed.), *Urban Achievement in Early Modern Europe: Golden Ages in Antwerp, Amsterdam and London*, Cambridge, 2001.
9. With regard to the impact and organization of borders in the Netherlands, see: B. De Ridder, *Lawful Limits. Border Management and the Formation of the Habsburg-Dutch Boundary, c. 1590–1665* (doctoral thesis, KU Leuven, 2016).
10. O. Gelderblom, *Cities of Commerce: the Institutional Foundations of International Trade in the Low Countries, 1250–1650*, Princeton, 2013.
11. J. Van Roey, 'Over mensen en dingen in onze gouden eeuw. Uit de Certificatieboeken van het Stadsarchief.', *Kroniek, orgaan van Stabuco*, 1951, pp. 24–6.
12. O. Gelderblom & R. Grafe, 'The Rise and Fall of the Merchant Guilds: Re-thinking the Comparative Study of Commercial Institutions in Premodern Europe', *Journal of Interdisciplinary History* 40, 2010, pp. 477–511.
13. A. M. Kint, 'The ideology of commerce: Antwerp in the sixteenth century', in: P. Stabel et al. (ed.), *International Trade in the Low Countries (14th-16th centuries): Merchants, Organisation, Infrastructure*, Leuven, 2000, pp. 213–22.
14. Stadsarchief Antwerpen (SAA), Certificatieboeken (Cert) 6, Folium (fol) 410 v, 12 augustus 1547.
15. SAA, Cert 5, fol 206 r, 13 augustus 1542.
16. A clear description of the bills of exchange system can be found at the following website 'The Medieval Bill of Exchange': https://www.economics.utoronto.ca/munro5/BILLEXCH.htm [consulted 23 January 2020].
17. F. Trivellato, 'Merchants' Letters Across Geographical and Social Boundaries', in: F. Bethencourt & F. Egmond (ed.), *Correspondence and cultural exchange in Europe, 1400–1700*, Cambridge, 2007, pp. 80–103; R. A. Goldthwaite, 'The Practice and Culture of Accounting in Renaissance Florence', *Enterprise & Society* 16, 2015, pp. 611–47.
18. J. H. Munro, 'The Low Countries' Export Trade in Textiles with the Mediterranean Basin, 1200–1600: A Cost-Benefit Analysis of Comparative Advantages in Overland and Maritime Trade Routes', *International Journal of Maritime History* 11, 1999, pp. 1–30.
19. J. Puttevils & M. Deloof, 'Marketing and Pricing Risk in Marine Insurance in Sixteenth-Century Antwerp', *The Journal of Economic History* 77, 2017, pp. 796–837.
20. W. Brulez, 'L'Exportation des Pays-Bas vers l'Italie par voie de terre, au milieu du XVIe siècle', *Annales. Économies, Sociétés, Civilisations* 14, 1959, pp. 461–91.
21. Sabbatini, Cercar esca.
22. R. Baetens, *De nazomer van Antwerpens welvaart : de diaspora en het handelshuis De Groote tijdens de eerste helft der 17de eeuw*, Brussels, 1976.

"In stead of a companion, let the Traueller haue alwayes with him some good Booke in his pocket, as wee reade that *Alexander* the Great laied *Homer* vnder his pillow, and let this Booke be either such, as fits his ends or study, or such as containeth precepts or sentences, which by daily vse he desires to make familiar vnto him, alwaies bewaring that it treat not of the Commonwealth, the Religion thereof, or any Subiect that may be dangerous to him: By this companion he shall make the solitude of the Innes and many irkesome things lesse vnpleasing to him."

"So the Traueller [...] must carry onely most necessary things with him, especially in such places as the Low-Countries, where boates and waggons are changed many times in one dayes iourney, and where (as also in *Italy*) they bring him not to his Inne, but onely to the water side; or to the gates of the City: for in such places heauy carriages will be a great burthen or charge to him."

"Let him enquire after the best Innes [...] In the best Innes, with moderate and ordinary expences, he shall auoid the frauds and iniuries of knaues, and shall sleepe safely, both for his person and the goods hee hath with him. In all Innes, but especially in suspected places, let him bolt or locke the doore of his chamber: let him take heed of his chamber fellowes, and alwayes haue his Sword by his side, or by his bed side; let him lay his purse vnder his pillow, but always foulded with his garters, or some thing hee first vseth in the morning, lest hee forget to put it vp before hee goe out of his chamber."

"Some aduise that a Traueller should learne to swimme, but I thinke that skill is more for pleasure at home, then of vse abroade, and yeelds small comfort or helpe in a storme at Sea. [...] In like manner some perswade a Traueller to vse himselfe first to hardnesse, as abstaining from wine, fasting, eating grosse meates, and going iournies on foote. But in my opinion, they shall better beare these things when necessity forceth, who cherish their body while they may. Neither doe I commend them, who in forraigne parts take iournies on foote, especially for any long way. Let them stay at home, and behold the World in a Mappe, who haue not meanes for honest expences; for such men, while they basely spare cost, doe so blemish their estimation, as they can enioy no company, but that of such poore fellowes as goe on foote with them, who can no way instruct them, or better their vnderstanding. [...] But for my part, I thinke the best going on foote, is [...] when a man leades his horse in his hand, and may mount him at pleasure."

A 16th-century Journey Planner

—

Hubert Meeus
Full Professor of Early Modern Dutch Literature and Theatre History, University of Antwerp

Travelling in the 16th century was no picnic. The roads were in a deplorable condition, vehicular transport provided little comfort and the traveller had to exercise all due patience. Hygiene and the quality of food in the inns were nothing to write home about either. In short, very few people embarked on a journey for their pleasure. There was also little information available to those intent on travelling despite the difficulties. Potential travellers turned to information obtained by word of mouth or to the travel journals kept by those who had gone before them.

Sommaire description de la France, Allemagne, Italie & Espagne

A measure of improvement was brought to this situation in the second half of the 16th century. In 1591, for example, a booklet was published in Geneva in sextodecimo printing format with the expansive title: *Sommaire description de la France, Allemagne, Italie & Espagne, avec la gvide des chemins pour aller & venir par les prouinces, & aux villes plus renommées de ces quatre regions. A quoy est adiousté vn recueil des foires plus celebres presque de toute l'Europe. Et vn traicté des monnoyes & leur valleur esdicts pays, prouinces & villes. Plus trois tables tres-amples: Le tout recueilli pour la commodité des voyageurs.*[1] It was a travel guide that also provided an overview of trade fairs and a treatise on monetary systems and rates of exchange, clearly aimed at the merchant class.

In the dedication to "Jean Pournas, seigneur de la Piemente" and signed by "Vostre humble cousin & serviable amy, Théodore de Mayerne Turquet" on 12 June 1591, the author points out that travellers driven by curiosity or the hope of material gain will accept the testing circumstances. A refugee, compelled to travel out of necessity, sees this quite differently. Whatever the reason for setting out on a journey, it is always a great comfort when – as if heaven sent – travellers meet with a good guide. In actual fact, acting as a guide is a duty of charity incumbent on all.[2]

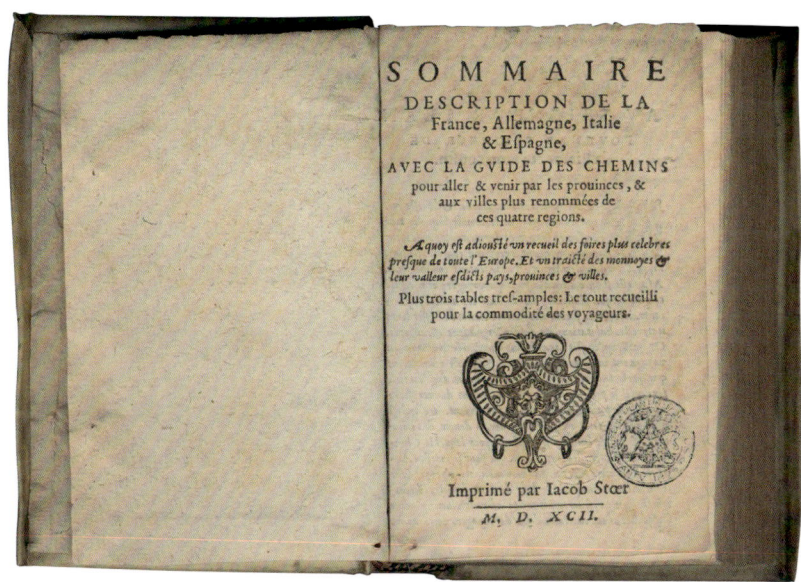

01 *Sommaire description de la France, Allemagne, Italie & Espagne.* Geneva, 1592, *1r (title page). Museum Plantin-Moretus, B 1465.

02 *Sommaire description de la France, Allemagne, Italie & Espagne.* Geneva, 1592, *1v-*2r (dedication). Museum Plantin-Moretus, B 1465.

The author, Théodore de Mayerne Turquet

The title page does not supply an author. In 1591, Théodore de Mayerne Turquet's name was not yet an argument that could be used to promote the booklet's sale, nor to lend it authority. Mayerne was born in Geneva on 28 September 1573. His father, Louis Turquet, had fled Lyon as a Calvinist to escape the persecution that had begun on 24 August 1572 with the St. Bartholomew's Day Massacre in Paris. In March 1573, he and his pregnant wife settled in Geneva. Louis, who in 1586 published a history of Spain, adopted the pen-name *de Mayerne-Turquet*.[3]

Théodore de Mayerne studied in Heidelberg from 1588 to 1591. Back in Geneva, his father, who had helped with writing the *Sommaire description*, led him to get the book published. The travel guide was an interim project for Théodore, because he enrolled on 25 October 1592 as a medical student at the University of Montpellier from which he graduated with his diploma in 1596.[4] He became one of the most renowned doctors of his time, albeit a controversial one, being at the heart of heated medical disputes in Paris. Despite this, he was promoted to the rank of personal physician to Henry IV, the king of France, and to James I and Charles I, kings of England. In 1629, at the English royal court, he met Peter Paul Rubens, who painted his portrait.[5] Virtually all his patients were famous people of the time, but his own renown also brought him many enemies. He died in Chelsea (London) in 1655.[6]

His sources

Although Mayerne had already travelled to Heidelberg before reaching the age of eighteen, that journey had definitely not furnished him with the experience necessary for writing a travel guide to Western Europe as soon as 1591. Consequently, his father is sure to have provided him with considerable assistance.[7]

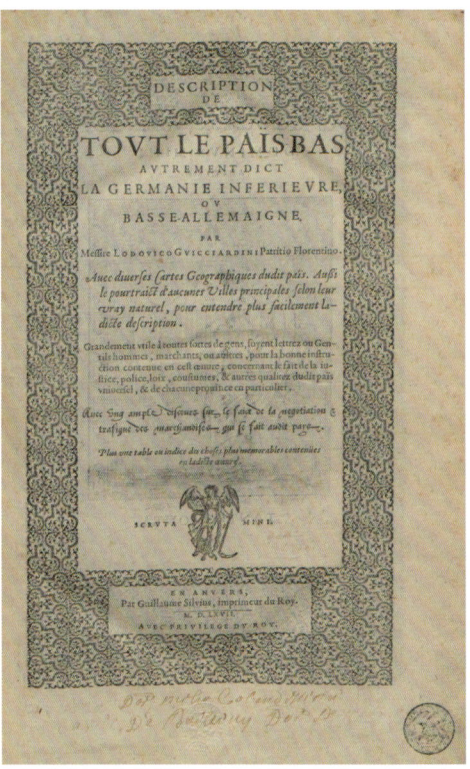

03 Ludovico Guicciardini, *Description de tout le Païs-Bas autrement dict la Germanie Inferieure, ou Basse-Allemaigne*. Antwerp, 1567. (Title page) Museum Plantin-Moretus, A 3165.

However, Mayerne had no hesitation either in borrowing information, although without taking pains to cite his sources. For example, he was able to make use of existing chorographies (descriptions of countries and regions), such as Lodovico Guicciardini's description of the Netherlands. Alongside maps, the atlases produced by Ortelius always contained a description of the depicted country or district as well. Prior to 1591, there already existed comprehensive descriptions of the regions of Germany, the Alps and Switzerland.[8]

A direct predecessor to his work was Charles Estienne's *La Guide des Chemins de France* (Paris, 1552). Alongside a geographical description of France, the work contains itineraries, with lists of cities, towns, castles, abbeys, rest stops and widely known sites of interest.[9] Estienne employed itineraries, such as the *Brugse Wegwijzer* ('Bruges Itinerary'), but he also sought information from merchants, envoys and pilgrims.[10] Now and then this approach created problems relating to the correct spelling of place names, as they had often been pronounced in a form of local dialect. Moreover, typesetters also made errors from time to time concerning the sequence of places, or else they would miss out a city and give routes inexplicable courses in the process, making the calculation of distances unreliable.[11] Seventeen editions of the guide were published up to 1623. Mayerne simply adopted Estienne's mistakes and typesetting errors without critical reappraisal, but in turn he did also add a number of his own itineraries, including the route from Antwerp to Metz.[12]

A practical travel guide

The focus of the *Sommaire description* is above all on practicality. Owing to its compact size, the 336-page booklet took up little space, which allowed travellers to carry it with them on their journeys with ease. This practical approach can be seen at once from the work's index of regions and provinces, markets, roads, rivers, lakes and currencies which could be consulted quickly and simply.

This is followed by a brief description of France, the Holy Roman Empire, Italy and Spain, in which Mayerne discusses practically all of Western Europe with the exception of Great Britain. Given that he shared his father's French nationality, it is little surprise that France should be accorded the greatest attention. In his historical overview, Mayerne takes a great leap back into the past to the foundation of the Frankish Empire, which formed one unified whole under Charlemagne, but which afterwards split into three parts, each of which in turn became fragmented into much smaller territories. Mayerne also draws attention to a number of regions such as Flanders and Brabant, which had formerly been part of France, but which in his time no longer recognized the French crown. He describes the various regions in France, starting out from Paris, the centre of power, money, law, knowledge and scholarship, and into which all wealth flowed. From the Île-de-France, he describes successively all of its surrounding regions and in such brevity that it comes across as a list. Proceeding region by region, he mentions the important cities, agricultural produce, and their ranking in the church hierarchy, such as bishopric or archbishopric. He locates cities in relation to rivers, because these were often the best means of connection.

In respect of the Netherlands, he points out its many densely populated cities. Ghent was then the most important city in Flanders, and it was clear that the glory days of Bruges lay in the past because the former trading city was placed in one line with Ypres, Kortrijk, Oudenaarde, Armentières and Douai. Flanders had no port, apart from Sluis, which had been destroyed several times.

In Brabant the situation was different. The most important city in the Low Countries was Antwerp on the River Scheldt: large, very wealthy and strong, with the largest number of merchants in Europe. Also worthy of note were the University of Leuven, Mechelen on account of its parliament, and Vilvoorde on account of its prison.

Most cities are mentioned without any further information. On occasion, Mayerne emphasizes one aspect. For example, Tournai had major manufacturers; Mariembourg and Philippeville were defensive forts against France; Leiden had a university; The Hague was a large village of more than 2000 houses; Rotterdam was the birthplace of Erasmus, and Liège had been destroyed by Charles the Bold. Mayerne distinguishes between three languages in the Low Countries: French, Flemish and Low German, and in various places two of these were spoken.

He pays little attention to sites of special interest. At times he does refer to remains from antiquity, such as the Roman theatres in Orange and Nîmes, and the Pont du Gard. The Château de Chambord and the bridges at Avignon and Prague also get a mention. There are rarely comments on landscape, except with regard to a few lakes and the fact that Dover can be seen from Calais.

He scarcely refers to the mountains in his description of Switzerland. In Germany, Nuremberg is afforded greater attention, being a city where many merchants had become established. Concerning points north and east, his descriptions extend to Gdansk, Bohemia, Moravia and Silesia.

In view of the fact that he had obtained almost all his information from elsewhere, he added hardly any personal reflections. He is more expansive on Lake Geneva, one of the largest lakes in Europe, than on Geneva itself, his place of residence. It is no coincidence that a more detailed entry is given to Lyon, with a reference to its Protestant church. Yet, although he had recently studied in Heidelberg, he tells us very little about it. As regards Montpellier, where he was intending to study, he comments only that the university is renowned for its teaching of medicine. His remark about the monasteries, that they are so wealthy that one "en est presque degousté" (p. 38), could have been made on account of his Calvinist views.

Itineraries

After the description of the various countries, there is an overview of the important itineraries in Western Europe. The custom of systematically depicting roads on maps took root only in the mid-18th century. The very first map to show roads was a small woodcut print of Central Europe, published in Nuremberg in 1501. The first map of France to display roads appeared in 1632, whereas the first map of England to do so came at the end of the 16th century.[13] The Museum Plantin-Moretus possesses a rare, four-part *Itinerarium Orbis christiani* dating from 1580 and with an Italian, German, French and Latin

04 *Itinerarium Orbis christiani.* (Title page of Part III). Museum Plantin-Moretus, R 13.34

title, but lacking any mention of the author, printer or place of publication. The maps were probably borrowed from an existing atlas, with the main routes being indicated on them using dotted lines.[14]

The itineraries are without doubt the most useful part of the *Sommaire Description*. The user is given a summarized list of the places successively encountered along the route, with the distances between them expressed in *lieues* (French leagues). The *lieue commune* is equivalent to 4.4454 km.[15] Splitting an itinerary into component routes enabled the traveller to choose for himself a combination of direct and alternative routes in order to reach his destination. Some routes are described in more detail than others. For example, there are routes in France where the distance between different places amounts to no more than one *lieue*, whereas for other routes the distances between places can be miles apart.

On occasion, Christophe Plantin would travel in person to Paris or Frankfurt, and in those specific cases the *Sommaire Description* would have recommended the following itineraries for him. The place names were often spelled according to how they sounded – or just misspelled – and identifying them correctly nowadays is not always straightforward.

The route suggested from Paris to Antwerp: Paris – Le Pont Yblon – Vaux de Relan [Vaudherland] – Louvres en Parisis [Louvres] – S. Ladre [?] – La Chapelle [-en-Serval] – Pont Harmen bois [Pontarmé] – Senlis – Saint Christophle – Pont-Sainte-Maxence – Gournay [-sur-Aronde] – Arçon sur Marc [Ressons-sur-Matz?] – Roye – Nesle – Licourt – Péronne – Cambrai – Haspres – Valenciennes – Cleuem [Cuesmes?] – Landere [?] – Chateau Chasteau [Casteau?] – Monsem [Mons?] – Tubeke [Tubize] – Brussels – Vilvoorde – Mechelen – Antwerp, "Ville de grand commerce": a total distance of 77 *lieues* (approximately 342 km).[16]

From Antwerp to Frankfurt via Mainz: Lier – Stingen [Itegem?] – Harsel [Herselt] – Diest – Hasel [Hasselt] – Mastrich [Maastricht] – Gulpen – Aix [Aachen] – Düren – Vitrich [Wichterich] – Ehendorff [Eckendorf] – Sensich [Sinzig] – Andernach – Canelius [Koblenz?] – Renes [Rhens] – Probhart [Boppard] – Vvesel [Oberwesel?] – S. Guoer [Sankt Goar] – Drechshause [Trechtingshausen?] – Bingen [am Rhein] – Mayence [Mainz] – Frankfurt: a total distance of 52 *lieues* (approximately 231 km).[17]

05 *Sommaire description de la France, Allemagne, Italie & Espagne*. Geneva, 1592, pp. 164-5. Museum Plantin-Moretus, B 1465.

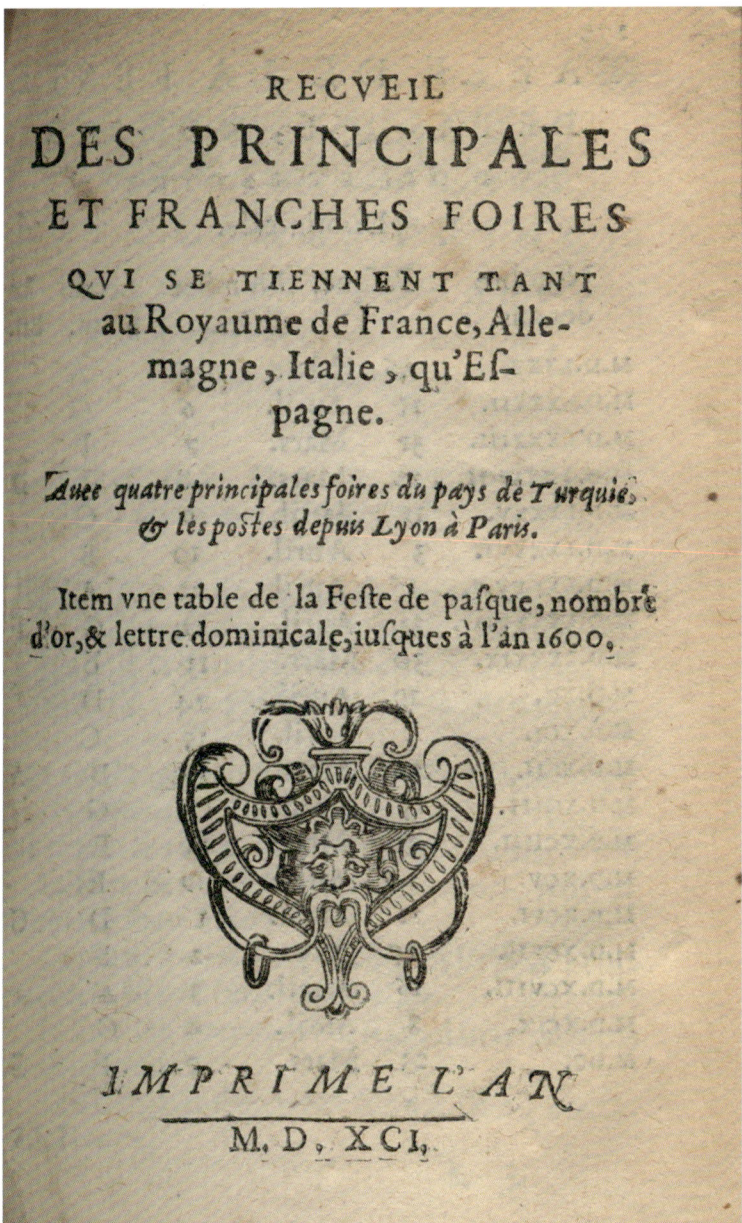

06 *Sommaire description de la France, Allemagne, Italie & Espagne.* Geneva, 1592, p. 271.
Museum Plantin-Moretus, B 1465.

Markets and rates of exchange

On page 271 the booklet has a new title page: *Recueil des principales et Franches Foires qui se tiennent tant au Royaume de France, Allemagne, Italie, qu'Espagne. Avec quatre principales foires du pays de Turquie et les postes depuis Lyon à Paris. Item une table de la Feste de pasque, nombre d'or, & lettre dominicale, iusques à l'an 1600.* The intention had not been to create a separate booklet at this point, because the page numbering and inscriptions are carried forward and the first title page had already introduced this section. Preceding this overview of the markets, there is a table showing the date of Easter, the golden ratio and the dominical letter from 1581 to 1600, because the date on which many markets were held depended on the date of Easter and other religious festivals, which varied from year to year. By his own admission, Mayerne had taken the information for this section from a German work of 1577, which explains why the list of Easter dates starts in 1581.[18] Mayerne continues by listing the important markets by country, including not only the larger cities, such as Bruges, Antwerp, Ghent, Brussels or Leuven, but also the smaller ones, such as Oudenburg, Harelbeke, Sint-Winoksbergen (Bergues, in France), Herentals, Mol or Aarschot. This inventory of markets is followed by a list of 39 stopovers on the post road from Lyon to Paris, each of which is an orderly distance of three *lieues* from the next.

Mayerne also adds to this a *Petit traité des metaux et monnoyes fort utile pour le voyager*. He points to the lack of order in the monetary system, attributable to the caprices of rulers and to the ignorance and avarice of the people, who increase the value of gold and silver recklessly. His information was not intended for speculators. He explains where different types of currency are accepted and then provides an overview of the monetary systems and rates of exchange in a number of German cities, concluding with Antwerp. A final table compares weights in other trading centres, such as Lyon, Paris, London, Frankfurt, Milan, Venice, etc., using 100 pounds in Antwerp as his benchmark.

The printer Jacob Stoer

Sommaire description was published in Geneva in 1591 by the printer Jacob Stoer (Etlingen 1542–Geneva 1610). The title page provides a comprehensive explanation of the booklet's contents, but it omits the author's name and place of publication. It is generally understood that Jacob Stoer printed works in Geneva, but it may be that in the case of this book – aimed at a wide audience of travellers – he did not wish to scare away potential Catholic buyers through any association with the "Rome of the Calvinists". Jacob Stoer arrived in Geneva on 15 April 1559. There, he became apprenticed to Jean Crespin, learning the trade of typesetter at the latter's printing firm. After 1571 he set up in business for himself. The mainstay of his endeavours focused on religious works and editions of works by classical authors, later including legal and scientific works as well. Through this, he built up a very diverse body of work that allowed him to serve a broad spectrum of buyers. With 368 titles to offer, he was one of the most important printer-publishers in Geneva.[19]

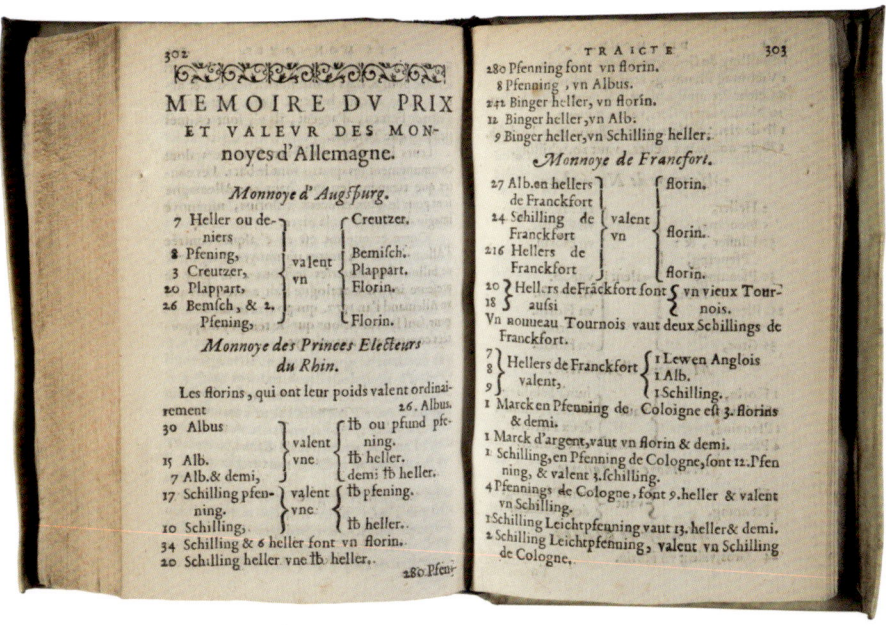

07 *Sommaire description de la France, Allemagne, Italie & Espagne.* Geneva, 1592, p. 302.
Museum Plantin-Moretus, B 1465.

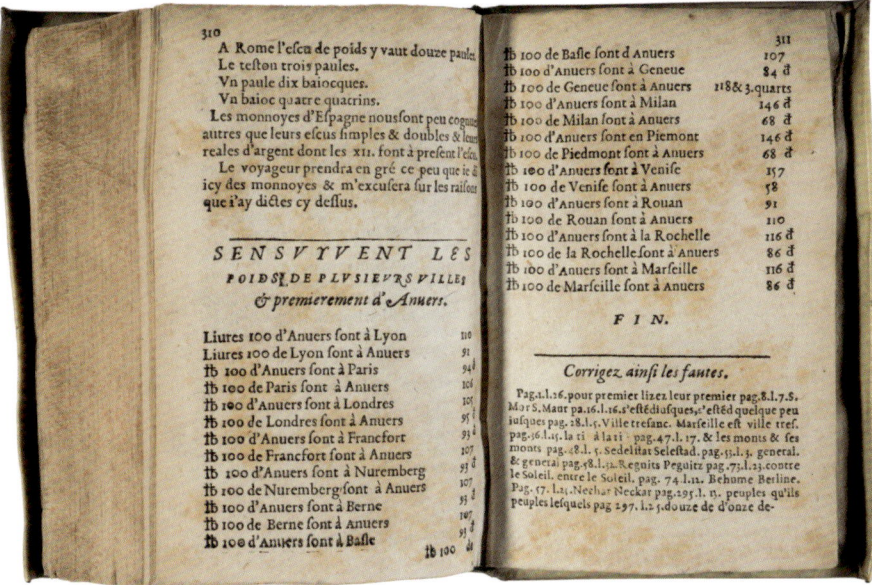

08 *Sommaire description de la France, Allemagne, Italie & Espagne.* Geneva, 1592, p. 310-11.
Museum Plantin-Moretus, B 1465.

Editions

Although Mayerne could not boast of its great originality, his booklet did enjoy success, as he had collected and compiled material that covered virtually all of Western Europe. The number of copies from the first print run is unknown, but Stoer reprinted an identical version in 1592. Moreover, a reprint in duodecimo format is known to have been made in Lyon in 1596.[20]

In 1604, Jean Petit and Claude le Vilain brought a new edition in duodecimo onto the market in Rouen. The two printers probably worked in collaboration, dividing the print run between themselves. They brought the year of its dedication up-to-date, changing 1591 to 1603.

The competition in Rouen seems to have had an inspirational effect, because Jacob Stoer printed a new edition as early as 1605, this time in Cologny, a municipality near Geneva to which he had moved in order to avoid the ban by the French government on the distribution of books from Geneva. Stoer also amended the Easter table so that the dates ran from 1605 to 1620. Jacob Stoer's successors reprinted the booklet yet again in 1611 and 1618.

The Rouen edition also enjoyed success, given that Claude Le Vilain brought the work back to the printing presses in 1606, 1614, 1615, 1624, 1629 and 1640, each time with an amended table for the Easter dates. In 1642, Clement Malassis made the last reprint of the work to be produced in Rouen. The very last edition to be printed anywhere was in 1653 in Geneva.[21]

Selective bibliography

Biervliet, Lori van, 'Duitse reisroutes als studiebron voor de Brugse wegwijzer van 1380–1400', *Biekorf* 83, 1983, pp. 97–110.

Broc, Numa, *La géographie de la Renaissance (1420–1620)*. Paris, 1980.

Fordham, H. George, 'The earliest French itineraries 1552 and 1591: Charles Etienne and Théodore de Mayerne-Turquet', *Transactions of the Bibliographical Society*, 4th series, 1920–21, pp. 193–224.

Mączak, Antoni, *De ontdekking van het reizen: Europa in de vroeg-moderne tijd*. Utrecht, 1998.

Stagl, Justin, *A History of Curiosity: the Theory of Travel, 1550–1800*. London, 2006.

Sweet, Rosemary, Gerrit Verhoeven & Sarah Goldsmith (red.), *Beyond the Grand Tour: Northern Metropolises and Early Modern Travel Behaviour*. London, 2017.

Trevor-Roper, Hugh, *Europe's Physician: the Various Life of Sir Théodore de Mayerne*. New Haven (Connecticut), 2006.

Verhoeven, Gerrit, *Anders reizen? Evoluties in vroegmoderne reiservaringen van Hollandse en Brabantse elites (1600–1750)*. Hilversum, 2009.

Endnotes

1. A copy of the second edition of 1592 can be found in the library of the Museum Plantin-Moretus with shelf mark B 1465. The work can be consulted digitally via DAMS https://dams.antwerpen.be/asset/Q2eHPNf-GUGNWrHsiYGt36JpF [24/01/2020].
2. Sommaire Description, fol. *1v-*2r.
3. Hugh Trevor-Roper, *Europe's Physician: the Various Life of Sir Théodore de Mayerne*. New Haven (Connecticut), 2006, pp. 6–18.
4. Ibidem, p. 27.
5. Frances E. Huemer, *The Portraits: Portraits Painted by Rubens in Foreign Countries*. [Corpus Rubenianum Ludwig Burchard 19:1] Brussels, 1977, cat. no. 46.
6. Trevor-Roper, *Europe's Physician*, pp. 7–8, 365.
7. Ibidem, p. 20.
8. Numa Broc, *La géographie de la Renaissance (1420–1620)*. Paris, 1980, pp. 99–103.
9. Ibidem, p. 104.
10. Ibidem, p. 105; Jean Bonnerot (ed.), Charles Estienne, *La guide des chemins de France*. Paris, 1935, p. 29.
11. Bonnerot, Estienne, pp. 6–8, 31–3.
12. Ibidem, pp. 17–18; Broc, *La géographie*, p. 105.
13. Herbert George Fordham, *Roads on English and French Maps at the End of the Seventeenth Century*. Southampton, 1926, p. 1.
14. Museum Plantin-Moretus: R 13.34.
15. Horace Doursther, *Dictionnaire universel des poids et mesures anciens et modernes, contenant des tables des monnaies de tous les pays*. Amsterdam, 1965, p. 210.
16. Sommaire Description, p. 161.
17. Ibidem, pp. 164–5.
18. Ibidem, p. 301.
19. Alain Dubois, 'Jacob Stoer (1542–1610), un éditeur et ses auteurs', in Alain Riffaud (ed.), *L'écrivain et l'imprimeur*. Rennes, 2010, pp. 75–93.
20. Jochen Hoock & Pierre Jeannin, *Ars mercatoria: Handbücher und Traktate für den Gebrauch des Kaufmanns, 1470–1820: eine analytische Bibliographie Band I. 1470–1600*. Paderborn, 1991, I, 140, M11.3.
21. Ibidem I, pp. 140–2, M11.14.

"The Traueller must haue great care to preserue his health. [...] But most of all is this care necessarie for a Traueller: for those that are sicke by the way, suffer many discommodities in all places, and our Country men in *Italy* and *Spaine* runne high dangers, where howsoeuer being in health, they may discreetly shunne the snares of the Inquisition. [...] Men ready to die can ill dissemble, neither is any waight so heauy, as that of a wounded conscience, wherewith if the sicke man bee so affected, as hee professeth himselfe to bee of the Reformed Religion, then the Phisition and the Apothecarie are forbidden to helpe him, [...] and if hee recouer, hee shall bee sure to bee brought into the Inquisition: but if hee die, his body shall be buried in the high-way, not in any Churchyard."

"I aduise the Traueller in generall to be so wary, as he aduenture not to doe any new thing, till the example of others giue him confidence. Let him reproue nothing in another mans house, much lesse in a strange Common wealth, in which kind it is not amisse to seeme dumb or tongue-tied, so he diligently imploy his eyes and eares, to obserue al profitable things. Let him be curteous, euen somewhat to wards the vice of curtesie, to his Host, the children, and his fellow soiourners in the house. I doe not aduise him to imitate them, who will put off their hat to a very Dog; for in all actions basenesse must bee shunned, and decency embraced, but it is veniall somewhat to offend in the better part, applying our selues to the diuers natures of men."

Cum fueris Romae, Romano viuito more,
Cum fueris alibi, viuito more loci.

Being at Rome, the Roman manners vse,
And otherwhere each places custome chuse.

Tant de payis, tant'de guises.

So many countries, so many customs.

Advice for Travellers by the Humanist Justus Lipsius:
Italy or "Rome n'est plus Rome"?

Jan Papy
Professor Ordinarius in Latin Language & Literature, KU Leuven

> Vagari, lustrare, discurrere quivis potest;
> pauci indagare, discere, id est, vere peregrinari
>
> *Whosoever might wander, traverse [terrain] or roam about,*
> *few can investigate, learn, that is to say, truly travel abroad*
>
> *Justus Lipsius*

The Italian and Grand Tours

"I cannot hold it against our good friend that he should speak of Italy with such rapture. I know well how it has been able to lift my own spirits! Indeed, I may venture it is only in Rome that I have felt what it is to be human. Never since have I attained those heights nor such a sense of joy. In fact, by comparison with what I felt in Rome, I have never afterwards been happy again." It was with this personal outpouring of sentiment in dialogue with his friend Johann Peter Eckermann that Johann Wolfgang Goethe (1749–1832) looked back on his sojourn in the Eternal City following his *Italienische Reise* of 1786–88. If, for him, Rome had been the place where, at last, he "saw before him all the dreams of his youth as large as life" and where "his old conceits became so clear and alive, became so inextricably knit together, that they could advance as new", then the *Urbs* can be said to have exerted the same enduring fascination and appeal on artists, writers, philosophers and scholars alike, both in the centuries before Goethe and since.

If we imagine the Middle Ages as a time when it was chiefly traders, itinerant students and devoted pilgrims who were braving the many dangers of European routes to busy trading centres, important universities or prestigious sites of pilgrimage in Italy, then we can see how they were joined in the Renaissance and afterwards by new travellers: the art-aficionado writer seeking inspiration in the bustling cities and delightful vistas of the countryside, the artist inspired by literature who wished to observe and absorb the designs used in antiquity, and the scholarly humanist who wished to study and comprehend the sources of Ancient Rome.

These new travellers were no longer driven exclusively by *pietas* (piety) or other noble motives, but by *curiositas* (curiosity). As early as the Jubilee of 1350, although medieval pilgrims were still being guided through Rome by what was known as the *Mirabilia Urbis Romae* (Rome's oldest travel guide compiled without the pretence of scholarly accuracy and in which numerous stories of miracles were meant to inspire awe in pious believers), Francesco Petrarca (Petrarch) was already observing a change when visiting the Holy City of Rome:

> Instead of visiting churches out of Christian devotion, without paying heed to the salvation of their souls, they would rather traverse the city with the curiosity of poets [*curiositate poetica*]. Now, however delightful intellectual pursuits may be, they are – as it were – as nothing if they do not lead to the one great goal.[1]

Different motives were driving the new travellers. Some, such as Geoffrey Chaucer, were inspired by the example of Petrarch's visit to the city of Rome in 1341 on the occasion of his poet's coronation on the Capitoline Hill. Others had their 'poetic curiosity' aroused by new descriptions of the country, such as Leandro Alberti's comprehensive *Descrittione di tutta Italia* (1550) and the numerous travel journals which served up often adventurous and exotic

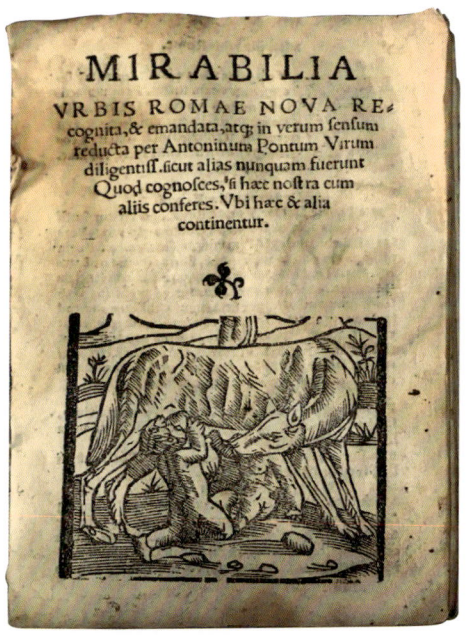

01 *Mirabilia Urbis Rome Nova Re* cognita & mandata, acque in veri Sensum reducta per Antonium Pontum, Rome, Antonius Bladus de Asula, 1524, in-32°. (Title page).
Universidad Complutense de Madrid, Biblioteca Historica Fondo Antiguo (F) – FLL 9512.[2]

details. An ever-growing series of professional reports written by diplomats, ambassadors and papal envoys, often scholar-humanists in public service who had been specially sent forth by their sovereign or country, awakened a thirst for travel and a curiosity about foreign parts, increasingly appealing to people's imaginations.

In the 16th century, and especially in its second half, the curiosity of visitors to Italy was actually steered in a well-defined direction: proper guidebooks were brought onto the market "on the art of travelling" (*De arte peregrinandi*) in

02 *View of Rome*, c. 1550. Map taken from Sebastian Munster, Cosmographia, Basel, Heinrich Petri, 1550.

which the novice traveller to Rome was informed at length and in detail about how, when, and where to travel in order to acquire as many (educational) benefits as possible and, quite besides that, in order to make as many praiseworthy observations during this – as ever – still precarious and costly endeavour. For the Renaissance traveller schooled in literature, the ode to the Homeric Ulysses by the Roman poet Horace acted as a paradigm (*Epistulae*, I, 2, 17–20):

Rursus, quid virtus et quid sapientia possit,
utile proposuit nobis exemplar Ulixen,

qui domitor Troiae multorum providus urbes,
et mores hominum inspexit, latumque per aequor,
dum sibi, dum sociis reditum parat, aspera multa
pertulit...

Again, of the power of worth and wisdom
he has set before us an instructive pattern in Ulysses,
that tamer of Troy, who looked with discerning eyes upon the cities
and manners of many men, and while for

self and comrades
he strove for a return across the broad seas, many hardships
he endured...³

Further to this, the acquisition of knowledge was meant to encompass more than academic knowledge alone; travel was of unique educational value, because on the one hand it succeeded in triggering curiosity, while on the other it was a necessary moral complement to and deepening of understanding, as regards literary instruction through the medium of books. Just as Ulysses through his contact with foreign peoples and customs had become a model of *virtus* and *sapientia* (virtue and wisdom), so the humanists in their educational programme also strove for a more wide-ranging knowledge of people, customs and social particularities as the objective of their travels. Similarly, Michel de Montaigne stated in his *Essais* (II, 10) that observation of the nature and condition of people and of the customs of different peoples was the true object of moral philosophy. This humanist objective of travel found another defender more than a century later in Jean-Jacques Rousseau and his work *Émile* (1762). When broaching the difficulties of travelling in this work, Rousseau presses his case: "Voyager pour voyager, c'est errer, être vagabond... Je voudrais donner au jeune homme un intérêt sensible à s'instruire."⁴

Moreover, to deepen this knowledge it had to be committed to the pages of a travel journal in writing. Not only did this bring systematic order to travelling and observation, but these written reflections also intensified and explored the intellectual pleasures and numerous aesthetic impressions enjoyed when on one's travels. For that matter, this systematic approach to travelling and observation was also to engender a new tradition. Michel de Montaigne kept a systematic travel journal in his *Journal de Voyage*. Pieter Cornelisz. Hooft (1581–1647) recorded his journey to Rome during the period 1598–1601 in his *Reis-Heuchenis*. Not only did he use it to summarize in chronological order the many antiquities that

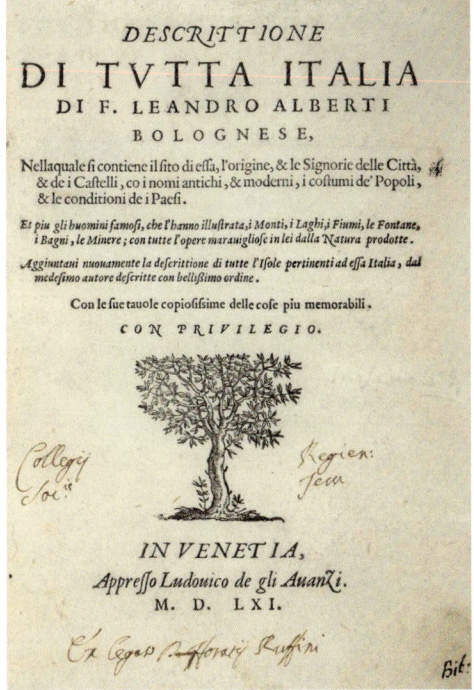

03 Leandro Alberti, *Descrittione di tutta Italia*, Venice, Giovanni Battista Porta, 1581, dedicated to the French rulers Henry II and Catherine de' Medici (first print-run in Bologna, 1550). Ten editions were published in Venice; two Latin editions were published in Basel.

he had personally seen along the way (in Lyon, Verona, and in Rome), but he also used it to discuss the many things that he had seen from the perspective of Rome's fall from greatness.

This, too, is understandable when considering the tradition of the Tour of Rome itself. It is the case that, alongside the aforementioned travel journals, countless poems were also in circulation that opined on the ruins, as well as on Rome's faded grandeur, in emotional and picturesque terms. Here, we are confronted with a new genre of poetry that had arisen in Italy as the result of a quite recent renewal of scholarly interest in the material remains of Ancient Rome. What is more, the genre proved highly successful both on the Italian peninsula and beyond. It can be said that more than one non-Italian poet felt moved to follow suit; in around 1500, the German humanist Conrad Celtes had already written a classical ode to the rubble of his "Germanic Rome", Trier, following the example of Italian humanists such as Cristoforo Landino and Enea Silvio Piccolomini, the later Pope Pius II. Still more famous are the French verses from the collection of sonnets *Antiquitez de Rome* (1558) by Joachim du Bellay in which the French Pléiade-poet imitated the five-year-older poem in Latin *De Roma* by the Palermitan poet Ianus Vitalis:

> Nouveau venu, qui cherches Rome en Rome,
> Et rien de Rome en Rome n'apperçois,
> Ces vieux palais, ces vieux arcz que tu vois,
> Et ces vieux murs, c'est ce que Rome on nomme...[5]

Thou stranger, which for Rome in Rome here seekest,
And nought of Rome in Rome perceiv'st at all,
These same old walls, old arches, which thou seest,
Old palaces, is that which Rome men call.
(Translation: Edmund Spenser, *The Ruins of Rome*, 1591)

Indeed, in around 1600, the aforementioned Hooft was also to express that same sentiment in his own poetic work:

> 'Toudt Rome leydt daer neer wel waerdich te beweenen,
> En van die grote naam siet men maer wenich steenen,
> Den hemel sloech het hooft en 't was des blixems buit,
> D'aert heeft de voet bewelt, de rest schuylt onder 't cruyt.

There she lies, old Rome, to be mourned with dignity,
And of that great name, nought is there to see but a few stones,
Heaven struck her head and 'twas the booty of the lightning bolt,
The earth did overlay her feet, the rest lies hid 'neath the weeds.

However, it was not only the evocative verses in this new "poésie des ruines" or the spicy – and, indeed, sometimes salient – travel journals that drew so many foreign writers and artists to the Eternal City. The etchings, drawings or paintings of famous *vedutisti*, such as Maarten

04 *A drawing of a new discovery, sent from Rome to Lipsius by his former pupil Johannes Hemelarius (1602): a statue of the Vestalis Maxima (Chief Vestal). The statue, according to Hemelarius, was included in the collection held by Cardinal Cesi. Pen and ink drawing, 275 × 175 mm. Museum Plantin-Moretus, M 157, fol. 73.*

van Heemskerk and Jan Gossaert, spurred dozens of painters, draughtsmen, etchers and sculptors to journey to the artistic centre to perfect their skills there and to study the new finds, often proudly displayed in rich collections, such as those held by the Barberini, Borghese, Chigi, Ludovisi or Pamphili families. Incidentally, both the artistic tradition and that of literary reporting were to have lasting repercussions. Up until the following century, spending time in southern Europe became an indispensable component of the *Bildungsgang* ('course of education') of a young painter or sculptor. The *Grand Tour*, which took shape in the first half of the 17th century, became one of the most important elements in the education of Europe's governing elite. Princes, nobility, statesmen and the clergy travelled throughout the continent. The underlying reason for these ventures continued to be linked to the humanist conception of travel, as attested in a letter of 1637 written by Papal Nuncio Visconti about King Ladislaus IV of Poland when he was still a prince and yet to inherit the throne:

> Owing to his travels through foreign countries in which he made comparison of foreign things with those matters of which he was familiar, he perfected his innate talents and enriched his soul with information on every subject.

The educational aspect of the Italian Tour would appear fundamental. This was certainly the view held by Christophe Plantin's personal friend Justus Lipsius (Overijse 1547–Leuven 1606). Even as a young philologist and humanist, his focus was already on the birthplace of the Renaissance and humanism, and he appraised his own Italian Tour for its educational value. For that reason, let us return to the Netherlands of the 16th century via Bertus Aafjes's *Een Voetreis naar Rome* (1946) and Goethe's *Italienische Reise* (1786–88).

05 Anonymous (Isaac Claesz. Swanenburgh(?), *Portrait of Justus Lipsius*, Leiden (?), 1585. Oil on panel (632 × 515 mm). Portrait donated to Balthasar Moretus by Johannes Woverius on 1 October 1620. Museum Plantin-Moretus, V.IV.94.

Lipsius in Italy and Rome

Unlike Erasmus, Lipsius had the opportunity of staying in Rome while still in his youth. Thanks to the involvement of Plantin, by whom he, as a precocious linguistic genius, had just had his first philological work published (*Variarum lectionum libri* IV), he was made secretary to Cardinal Granvelle in Rome. Unlike in the case of Erasmus, we do not read of any disillusionment or antipathy following Lipsius's sojourn in Rome (1568–70). His letters continually bring to the fore his nostalgic longing for Italy. In 1587, for example, Lipsius wrote to Janus Duystius: "Had I the youth and strength of yesteryear, then would I traverse my favourite places and embrace the men whose names invigorate me and give me new strength."[6] The same yearning is expressed in February 1592 in Lipsius's correspondence to Plantin's son-in-law, Franciscus Raphelengius: "In faith believe me, were my health and this body of mine but that much stronger, then would I cross the Alps swift-footed and leave behind these hateful intrigues."[7] Indeed, Lipsius added "[my love for] Italy exceeds that of all other countries"[8], and his love of that country never diminished[9], because it was "the fairest and most cultivated of them all."[10] His passion was such that at one time he even made serious attempts to become registered as a new Italian citizen in order to flee the ceaseless, disastrous warfare occurring in the Netherlands.[11]

It should come as no surprise that the focus of admiration for Italy and Rome expressed by Lipsius the antiquarian and philologist – just as that expressed by his predecessor and example Erasmus – was directed almost wholly towards Ancient Rome. As with the hurriedly erudite Erasmus, the humanist Lipsius confronts us with a form of wilful blindness common to humanists: looking with nostalgia and tears in their eyes at the ancient ruins of the once so magnificent Rome, but not at the radiant new culture of Rome contemporary to the 16th century. It is noteworthy, for example, how Lipsius was blind to the literary masterpiece of such a person as Torquato Tasso, to the wonderful polyphony of Giovanni Perluigi da Palestrina, or to the architectural gems by Michelangelo or Vignola. In his correspondence with Roman humanists and cardinals in subsequent years, he made no mention of the imposing construction projects by the architect Domenico Fontana during the *Roma felix* of Pope Sixtus V: the dome of St. Peter's Basilica, the extension of the Vatican library, the laying out of public parks and broad, straight paved streets intended to link the principal churches in Rome, the memorable erection of the obelisk in St. Peter's Square, the building of numerous fountains to provide the populace with water thanks to reconstruction of the Roman aqueduct dating to Emperor Severus Alexander …, there appeared to be no room for these things in the mental universe of the humanist Lipsius.

In the footsteps of Erasmus and other humanists, and before anything else in contemporary Italy, Lipsius sought out Rome's bygone glory, its *magnitudo*. This explains, for example, Lipsius's quasi-lyrical evocation of his visits to Lake Trasimeno, Cannae, Alba Longa, Tibur (Tivoli) and Baiae. For him, Italy was synonymous with retrieving reminiscences of its glorious past: a visit to Pliny's villa, beholding the remains of the villas owned by Cicero and Varro, casting his antiquarian gaze over the remnants of temples, theatres, triumphal arches, tombs or inscriptions;

06 *Rome, Baths of Caracalla*, c. 1575
Etching (375 × 210 mm) from Étienne Dupérac, *I vestigi dell'antichità di Roma: Vestigij delle Terme di Antonino Caracalla ...* Rome, Lorenzo Vaccari, 1575.

it was this that stimulated Lipsius's vivid imagination and aroused his scholarly interest.[12] The same imagination of someone fully absorbed by the ancient world was also the foundation for the literary expression of Lipsius's Roman Tour: the *Admiranda sive de Magnitudine Romana*, printed in 1598 by Jan Moretus at the *Officina Plantiniana* (Plantin Press), it was a series of dialogues concerning the grandeur and might of Rome. It is striking that, even in the introductory chapter to this *Admiranda* (I, 1), it is once again underlined how Ancient Rome continued to live on for humanists such as Lipsius: "In fact, these broken and crumbled constructions are still steeped in the spirit of Ancient Rome."

Therefore, contemporary Italy was of importance only insofar as it was able to bring the studious Lipsius in contact with other celebrated scholars of Classical Antiquity, such as Carlo Sigonio and Marc Antoine Muret (Muretus). Besides, Lipsius also sensed a decline in Italian humanism, which once had seemed to exert a monopoly over the liberal arts. As early as 1588, he wrote to the Florentine writer Jacopo de Corbinelli, then resident in Paris as tutor to the son of Catherine de' Medici, that he had always loved the Italian people, but above all those men most worthy of ancient Italy, such as Corbinelli himself. Sadly, Lipsius lamented at the end of his letter how Italy was no more.[13]

IVSTI LIPSI ADMIRANDA,

siue,

DE MAGNITVDINE ROMANA LIBRI QVATTVOR.

AD SERENISSIMVM PRINCIPEM
ALBERTVM AVSTRIVM.

ANTVERPIÆ,
EX OFFICINA PLANTINIANA,
Apud Ioannem Moretum.
M. D. XCVIII.
Cum Priuilegiis Cæsareo & Regio.

07 Justus Lipsius, *Admiranda sive de Magnitudine Romana libri quattuor*, Antwerp, Jan I Moretus, 1598, 4°. Museum Plantin-Moretus, A 2008.

Whereas Erasmus gave vent on several occasions to his profound disillusionment with Christian Rome, where, instead of apostles, princes of the Church lodged in marble palaces – a disillusionment that, at times, he generalized unjustly to include the Italians and Romans themselves – Lipsius believed, in full post-Tridentine Counter-Reformation style, that it was only through the Holy See that Rome could still retain something of Italy's bygone greatness. This is not to say that he regretted the *Urbs urbium*[14] having become the centre of Catholicism. He contended only that this was the sole lustre not to have been lost by Rome. The greatness of Rome, as he stated in the aforementioned *Admiranda* of 1598, had not become greater, but it had become better! Despite the Reformation – that division of Christian unity – this new Rome had succeeded in maintaining her "statut cosmique et solaire de maîtresse de l'univers".[15] Lipsius also made a clear distinction between Rome as the most admirable centre of the *Imperium Romanum* and Rome as the centre of the true faith[16] in a letter to his former student Johannes Baptista Baronius, when the latter had reached Rome in March 1603 together with Guillaume Richardot: "I am pleased that you are both come to Rome, once great, exalted and admirable, now holy, pious and venerable."[17] Lipsius even added to his letter a poem in Phalaecian hendecasyllables,[18] clearly another variant (with a negative connotation) on Janus Vitalis's celebrated poems of 1553, *Roma prisca* and *Roma instaurata*[19]:

Ergo vos habet illa magna Roma?
Florens olim opibus, superba tectis,
Laeta civibus? Urbium Urbs, et orbis
Princeps? olim ea, nunc modestiores
Inscribit titulos: pia atque sancta
Et sedes adeo ipsa sanctitatis.

Thus it is that you sojourn in mighty Rome,
once thriving by her riches, splendid with her buildings,
fortunate in her citizens? City of cities, and first city of the world? Such honorary titles she once bore, but now
she bears those of more modest station: pious and holy,
and the seat itself of holiness.

Lipsius's longing and nostalgia for Rome's faded glory were clearly colliding with his personal experience of a slowly crumbling Roman humanism. As Lipsius saw it, Italy's few shining lights were not sufficient to maintain the vitality of its intellectual life. In particular, philology and literature were no longer at the level attained a century earlier. Moreover, although Lipsius was not inclined towards nationalism, nevertheless he subscribed to the following prevailing view as expressed by Erasmus:

Roma Roma non est, nihil habens praeter ruinas.

Rome is Rome no more; it has nothing but ruins.[20]

The verdict "Rome, n'est plus Rome"[21] began to be heard ever more vociferously from northern Europe. Italy and, above all, Rome, the *caput mundi* since the Middle Ages and the reborn centre of Rome's glory in the Renaissance, was still of interest only for its legendary treasures now held in its libraries and museums. For Europe's intellectual elite, the Roman Tour was no longer the indispensable tool in fashioning a sound, erudite education. When Lipsius asserts that Italy is no longer "the nursemaid of the manners and knowledge of antiquity",[22] we then see in him a double disillusion: firstly, in the faded 'philological' and 'intellectual' aura of an Italy once so much at the forefront; secondly, in the moral decay among the Italian people. The specific characteristics of the Italian people had been nation-bound and determined by climatological circumstances. In a celebrated letter to Philippe de Lannoy, with its focus on "methodical travel to Italy", Lipsius discusses in detail the various national character traits and their specific faults. This letter of 1578, which was reprinted several times, often separately, and also translated into English (1592) and French (1619), was the progenitor of the many 17th and 18th-century travel guides for Italy. Lipsius's warning to his pupil De Lannoy is illuminating:

> So, you are thinking of travelling to France? There, you shall also encounter frivolity and vanity, qualities that are most prevalent among this people (I might venture to say, unjustly, among all of them). Or to Italy? Tempestuousness and passion. To Spain? A certain pride and African haughtiness. To Germany? Banquets and drunkenness.[23]

Moreover, Lipsius brands the Italians as wily and artful, and in his eyes they are the most cunning of hypocrites.[24] Where Erasmus had already warned that journeys to the Eternal City were corrupting the morals and integrity of the young, Lipsius reprised the vision – he was joined in this by all Protestant Europe, which believed that papist Italy could be perceived a country of moral and religious perversity. Lipsius also followed the explanation made by Erasmus for this development: the negative influence of miscegenation in the final centuries before the fall of the Roman Empire, when Gallic and German tribes penetrated the Italian peninsula. Above all, the settlement of barbarian tribes such as the Goths and Vandals had given rise to a visible lowering of standards in public morality. Therefore, all visitors to Italy needed to be on their guard for the pernicious morals of the Italian people.[25]

The greatest danger that awaited the foreigner was that of Italian women. Almost invariably when Lipsius imparted valuable information to pupils or friends considering an *Iter italicum*, he warned them of the beautiful, but peculiarly licentious and shameless Roman and Venetian "Venuses". Lipsius's tart conclusion in a letter to his pupil Johannes ab Hollant was that a sojourn in Italy implied there were "no roses without thorns."[26] In an elegiac poem to his friend Janus Lernutius, he warned him of "Venus who reigns in Aeneas's city."[27] In the aforementioned letter to his pupil De Lannoy, he explains that their charm is such that one must not only exercise caution, but also have a good dose of luck in order to circumvent such a Scylla and Charybdis.[28]

Lipsius and the educational value of the Italian Tour: the ruins as a lesson in morality

The old debate about whether a journey to Italy yielded more in the way of pleasure (*voluptas*) than it did useful, instructive experience (*utilitas*) was one that flared up in the 16th century and continued unabated until the 18th. In England, for example, Roger Ascham's influential treatise *The Scholemaster* (1570) relates in plain terms that Ascham, while residing in Venice for nine days in 1552, "saw in that little time, in one city, more liberty to sin than ever I heard in our noble city of London in nine years." A French pamphlet by François Hotman dating from 1575 described the new phenomenon of "Italogalli" (young Frenchmen who had been corrupted through their contact with Italian morals and were now "befouling" all France) as the cause of the new faults that had taken root in France: treachery, faithlessness, sloth, godlessness, superstition and, as a consequence thereof, sodomy.[29]

Yet, deeply rooted though the time-worn spectres may have been of the "Anglus Italizatus, demon incarnatus" ("the Italianized Englishman, the devil incarnate") in England[30] or of the "Italogallus" in France, humanists such as Lipsius kept seeing unique and valuable educational opportunities in journeys to Italy and Rome. Lipsius showed continued enthusiasm in sending his own pupils to study there.

The explanation for this lies in Lipsius's role as the mentor of a prestigious *contubernium*,[31] where he tutored young men from prominent Catholic families who supported Spanish interests in the Southern Netherlands – among them, Plantin's grandson Balthasar Moretus and the brother of Peter Paul Rubens, Philip Rubens. For Lipsius, the matter central to this was in educating these young men to become responsible adults fit to take on positions of authority. Given his conviction that travelling and studying abroad was of the utmost importance educationally, Lipsius took the greatest care to maintain his Roman contacts in order to have his *contubernales* (students) introduced to a range of Roman *nobiles* and cardinals. However – wholly in line with Stoic philosophy – these journeys had to be "methodical" and "productive", yielding both *utilitas* and *voluptas* in the process.[32]

Lipsius first elaborated this insight in his aforementioned letter of 1578 to Philippe de Lannoy,[33] reprising the insight repeatedly in numerous letters to his pupils;[34] they were to develop their *prudentia* and *virtutes*, their practical wisdom and moral conduct in life by becoming acquainted with the manners of other peoples. For Lipsius the antiquarian, Italy, and above all Rome, remained the prime choice as a destination, because the Eternal City was and continued to be the *compendium* of the world, a city common to the whole world, the crowning glory and zenith of everything, a true miracle.[35] Moreover, despite the danger and sin in this Rome, as a centre of Christendom it was still invaluable for education and study.

What is more, the ultimate goal of travelling (*finis, scopum*) and the full-fledged fruit of this endeavour (*fructus*) could be best achieved by a visit to Italy. Pleasure (*voluptas*) was so easily encountered in that country that Lipsius's pupils (developing young adults strengthened by moral virtues) could shun it by the simplest means. Just as for Ulysses, they had to learn to bypass the pitfalls and remain deaf to the Sirens' enticements. Further to this, the usefulness (*utilitas*) of such a "reasoned" visit lay in the acquisition of genuine and steadfast virtuousness by becoming acquainted with foreign climes and customs.[36] Keeping their ears closed, their open eyes would be all the more likely to look around! Moreover, such a journey did not have to last all that long;[37] it was merely a *passage à la vie adulte* for his adolescents: Rome had to be *visited*, not inhabited. And, just as for Ulysses, a return to the mother country was

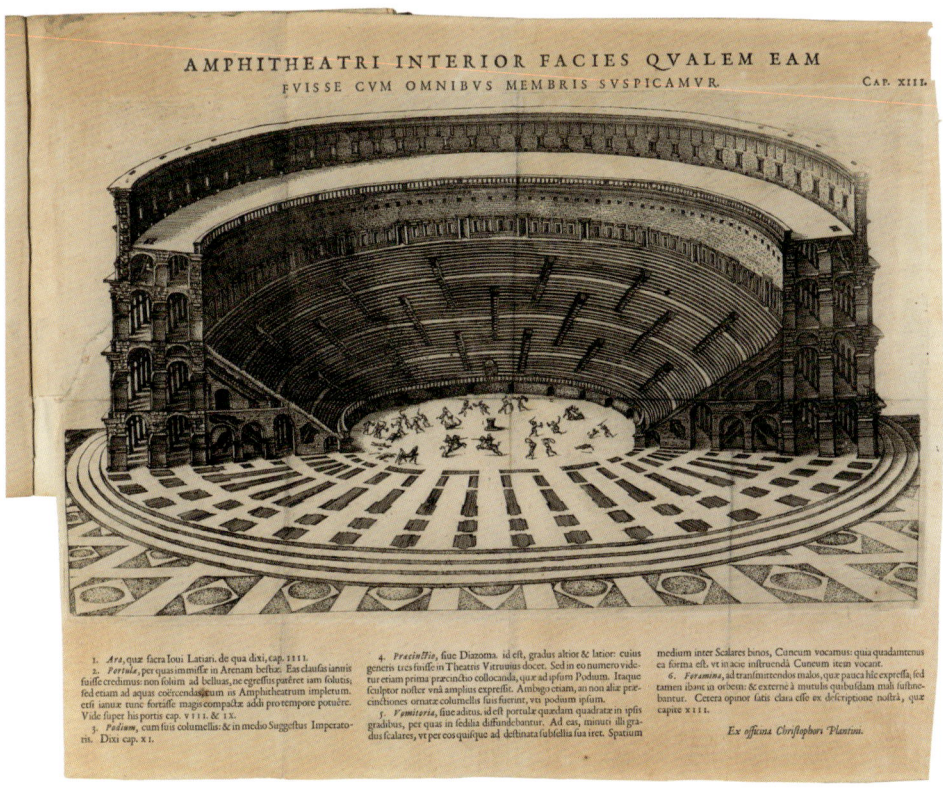

08 Engraving of the Colosseum from Justus Lipsius, *De amphitheatro liber*. Antwerp, C. Plantin, 1585, 4°. Museum Plantin-Moretus, A 1573.

self-evident; as fully formed, responsible adults they were expected to start a family and serve their home country. After all, lasting knowledge and true wisdom had yet to be gained through focused and intensive reading at home, without the attendant discomforts and dangers of travelling.[38]

Lipsius's own journey to Italy, and above all that to Rome, the centre of the Ancient Roman world, provided a solid basis for his further life as a scholar. Most of his important philological and antiquarian works were the result of his contacts with prominent Italian humanists, who also assured him access to their bountiful libraries and allowed him to see recent archaeological finds. Nonetheless, in the entry dedicating his work *De Amphitheatris* (1584) to Abraham Ortelius, Lipsius was forced to concede that his sojourn in Italy had not been to his complete satisfaction because he had then been too young to harvest the fruits of it.[39]

In that sense, Lipsius's own journey also serves as an example: in his case, too, he returned home to place himself at the disposal of his mother country.[40] Likewise, this is why he tutored his students in line with the Stoic ideal of rendering service to the state and humanity.[41] His own service in his lectures and works on various aspects of Ancient Rome consisted of instructing young men on the moral greatness (*magnitudo*) of the old Rome. However, in addition to being a historian, Lipsius was also a moralist. His personal motto *Moribus antiquis* ("to the ancient customs"), aptly taken by Lipsius from the Roman poet Quintus Ennius, is enough to show his preoccupation with Rome's great history,[42] because that great Rome had fallen into ruin and dust. As also evoked by Montaigne, it had become its own tomb.

Therefore, instead of a precise image, Lipsius can provide only "the image of the image": Rome as a model of fallen grandeur and as a lesson on vanity (*vanitas*),[43] because Rome is the whole world and the whole world is Rome. Thus the Rome of Lipsius is that of the *Antiquitez* by Joachim du Bellay: Rome as an image of all-devouring time, as an object in the hands of a capricious artist-God, as greatness and decay to the rhythm of the *fatum*. It is precisely for that reason that, for Lipsius, it could be a subject worthy of study for the young. In his poem on Italy to his friend Janus Lernutius, Lipsius was also of the view that it was in contemporary Rome that one had to seek the ideal Rome:

Et dices lacrumans:
in Roma quaerere Romam
Cogimur.

And, weeping, you say: we are compelled to seek out Rome in Rome.[44]

Selective bibliography

Chaney, E., *The Evolution of the Grand Tour. Anglo-Italian Cultural Relations since the Renaissance*. London–New York, 1998.

Enenkel, K.A.E., P. Van Heck & B. Westerweel (ed.), *Reizen en reizigers in de Renaissance. Eigen en vreemd in oude en nieuwe werelden*. Amsterdam, 1998.

Enenkel, K.A.E., & J. L. De Jong (ed.), *Artes Apodemicae and Early Modern Travel Culture, 1550–1700*. Leiden–Boston, 2019.

Huber-Rebenich, G. & W. Ludwig (ed.), *Frühneuzeitliche Bildungsreisen im Spiegel lateinischer Texte*. Weimar–Jena, 2007.

Iusti Lipsi Epistolae, ed. A. Gerlo *et al*. Brussels, Paleis der Academiën, 1978– .

Laureys, M., '"The Grandeur that was Rome": Scholarly Analysis and Pious Awe in Lipsius's *Admiranda*', in: K. A. E. Enenkel *et al*. (ed.), *Recreating Ancient History: Episodes from the Greek and Roman Past in the Arts and Literature of the Early Modern Period*. Leiden–Boston–Cologne, 2001, pp. 123–46.

Nave, F. de (ed.), *Justus Lipsius (1547–1606) en het Plantijnse Huis*. Antwerp, 1997.

Papy, J., 'Justus Lipsius, Rome en de Romereis: zoektocht naar een oude mythe?', *Kleio. Tijdschrift voor oude talen en antieke cultuur* N.R. 26, 1997, pp. 111–26.

Papy, J., '*Italiam vestram amo supra omnes terras*! Lipsius' Attitude towards Italy and the Italian Humanism of the late 16th Century', *Humanistica Lovaniensia* 47, 1998, pp. 245–77.

Warneke, S., *Images of the Educational Traveller in Early Modern England*. Leiden–New York–Cologne, 1995.

Lipsius's letter about the visit to Italy, addressed to Philippe de Lannoy, has now been translated in full into Dutch: *Justus Lipsius, Brieven aan studenten: De Romereis – Honden en geleerden – Drinkebroers en smulpapen*. Translation: Jan Papy. Leuven, Uitgeverij P, 2006.

Endnotes

1. Francesco Petrarca, *Epistolae de rebus familiaribus*, XII, 7.
2. The text of the popular guide *Mirabilia Urbis Romae*, written in around 1143 by Benedictus, a canon at St. Peter's in Rome, has been passed down to us separately and appears in miscellanies. Customarily, this pilgrim's guide was divided into a history of Rome and a section on architecture and sights of interest. The text has been copied, expanded, translated and reprinted many times.
3. Horace, *Satires, Epistles and Ars Poetica*. ed. and transl. H. Rushton Fairclough. London–Cambridge, Massachusetts, 1929, pp. 263–5.
4. Jean-Jacques Rousseau, *Émile*, M. Launay (ed.). Paris, 1966, p. 596.
5. *Antiquitez de Rome*, I, 3, v. 1–4.
6. *Iusti Lipsi Epistolae* (= *ILE*) II, 87 06 01 D (= *Cent. misc.* II, 38).
7. *ILE* V, [92] 01 08 R.
8. *ILE* IV, 91 04 14 M (= *Cent. Ital.*, 1): "Italiam vestram amo supra omnes terras."
9. *ILE* V, 92 06 23 M (= *Cent. Ital.*, 7): "Ego Italiae amorem non exui."
10. *ILE* 02 10 05 B (= *Cent. misc.* IV, 37): "Talis Italia erit, o pulcherrima et cultissima terrarum!"

11 *ILE* 04 09 19 (= *Cent. misc.* V, 54).
12 *ILE* I, 78 04 03 (= *Cent. misc.* I, 22), letter containing advice from Lipsius to Philippe de Lannoy, who was wishing to travel to Italy. This celebrated letter was reprinted several times and translated into English (1592) and French (1619). Lipsius's letter is thus also the progenitor of the many 17th and 18th-century travel guides for Italy. See L. Schudt, *Italienreise im 17. und 18. Jahrhundert*. Vienna, 1959, pp. 136–7.
13 *ILE* III, 88 04 00 C (= *Cent. misc. II*, 5): "Gentem vestram amavi semper et ex ea illos maxime, qui veteri illa Italia digni ... O Italia, Italia illa prisca, ubi es?"
14 Lipsius uses this honorary title in *ILE* V, 92 07 16 (= *Cent. Ital.*, 3). In *ILE* VIII, 95 10 24 S (= *Cent. Ital.*, 36) and *ILE* 99 04 30 B (= *Cent. Ital.*, 73) he refers to Rome as the *Urbs domina*.
15 J. Solé, *Les mythes chrétiens de la Renaissance aux Lumières*. Paris, 1979, p. 94.
16 *ILE* XIII, 00 02 07 S (= *Cent. Ital.*, 85): "Romae, id est, in luce illa gentium, in arce olim imperii, nunc pietatis."
17 *ILE* 03 03 16 B (= *Cent. misc.* V, 18): "Gaudeo Romam venisse, illam olim magnam, augustam, super-admirandam; nunc sanctam, religiosam, venerandam."
18 This metre had been employed by the Greek lyric poets Sappho and Anacreon; in Latin literature, it was chiefly Catullus and also subsequently the epigrammatic poet Martial who were renowned for poetry in this metre. The rhyme scheme was: – – | – ˘ ˘ | – ˘ | – ˘ | – ˘ (with possible substitution of the trochee (– ˘) for a spondee (– –) in the last metrical foot).
19 G. H. Tucker, *The Poet's Odyssey. Joachim du Bellay and the Antiquitez de Rome*. Oxford, 1990, pp. 104–11.
20 Erasmus, *Ciceronianus*, A. Gambaro (ed.). Brescia, 1965, p. 262.
21 F. Simone, 'Rome n'est plus Rome: un thème de la crise selon le témoignage des humanistes français', *Annales de l'Université Jean-Moulin. Langues étrangères* 2, 1975, pp. 99–109.
22 J. Jehasse, *La renaissance de la critique. L'essor de l'humanisme érudit de 1560 à 1614*. Saint-Étienne, 1976, p. 562; F. Waquet, *Le modèle français et l'Italie savante. Conscience de soi et perception de l'autre dans la République des Lettres (1660–1750)*. Rome, 1989, pp. 266–70.
23 *ILE* I, 78 04 03 (= *Cent. misc.* I, 22): "Galliam ecce cogitas? levitatem et vanitatem etiam, cum pleraque ea (omni, falso dicam) gente. Italiam? proterviam in ea et libidinem. Hispanias? typhum quemdam, et Africanum fastum. Germaniam? comessationes et ebrietatem."
24 *ILE* I, 78 04 03 (= *Cent. misc.* I, 22): "Nam et inter viros multi tecti, callidi, periti simulare."
25 Waquet, *Le modèle français*, p. 275; E. Giddey, 'Les conditions matérielles et spirituelles du voyage d'Italie à la fin du XVIe siècle et au début du XVIIe siècle', *Études de lettres* 3, 1960, pp. 173–95 (chiefly pp. 185–7); C. Howard, *English Travellers of the Renaissance*. London, 1914, pp. 54–66; L. Sozzi, 'La polémique anti-italienne en France au XVIe siècle', *Atti della Accademia delle Scienze di Torino. Classe di scienze morali, storiche e filologiche* 106, 1972, pp. 99–190 (chiefly pp. 99–108).
26 *ILE* 99 09 23 (= *Cent. Ital.*, 75), to his pupil Johannes ab Hollant: "quae bona et in rem tuam excerpe; cetera nec tange nec deliba, nam et rosis suae spinae adhaerent atque illas legere licet et ab his non laedi."
27 J. Lipsius, Elegia ad I. Lernutium De Urbe Roma, v. 30: "Et Venus Aeneae regnat in urbe sui". Full translation of this poem in J. Papy, 'Justus Lipsius, Rome en de Romereis: zoektocht naar een oude mythe?', *Kleio. Tijdschrift voor oude talen en antieke cultuur* N.R. 26, 1997, pp. 111–26.
28 *ILE* I, 78 04 03 (= *Cent. misc.* I, 22): "et inter feminas, formae conspicuae, sed lascivae et procaces. Non feminae, Veneres illae Romanae aut Venetae. Hic Scylla, ibi Charybdis; et duo haec discrimina ut enavigas, opus non prudentia quadam solum, sed dicam fortuna."
29 Sozzi, 'La polémique anti-italienne', p. 21.
30 S. Warneke, *Images of the Educational Traveller in Early Modern England*. Leiden–New York–Cologne, 1995, pp. 105–15; E. Chaney, *The Evolution of the Grand Tour. Anglo-Italian Cultural Relations since the Renaissance*. London–New York, 1998, and more specifically in his third chapter 'Quo vadis? Travel as Education and the Impact of Italy in the Sixteenth Century', pp. 58–100.
31 Originally, a *contubernium* was the smallest unit of soldiers in the Roman army: 8 legionnaires, equivalent to a modern squad. They would have shared a tent. The members of this unit were described as *contubernales*. In the context of Lipsius's students, this (military and Stoic) term refers to the select group of his students boarding in his house.
32 N. Doiron, *L'art de voyager. Le déplacement à l'époque classique*. Québec–Paris, 1995, pp. 17–32.
33 J. Stagl, 'Ars apodemica: Bildungsreise und Reisemethodik von 1560 bis 1600', in: X. von Ertzdorff–D. Neukirch–R. Schulz (ed.), *Reisen und Reiseliteratur im Mittelalter und in der Frühen Neuzeit*. Amsterdam–Atlanta, 1992, pp. 141–89; J. Stagl, *A History of Curiosity. The Theory of Travel 1550–1800*. Chur, 1995.
34 Thus, for example, *ILE* 99 01 03 (= *Cent. Germ.*, 48) to Johannes ab Hollant: "At ea familiarius iam paullo

nota, tum pedem proferre adsuadeam et Romam petere, illam olim et nunc (etsi in alia potentia) verticem et culmen rerum. Ibi, quidquid laudabile in orbe paene est, videre tibi fas in compendio."

35   *ILE* VIII, 95 05 01 C (= *Cent. Belg.*, I, 19): "compendium orbis"; *ILE* 99 01 03 (= *Cent. Germ.*, 48): "verticem et culmen rerum"; Lipsius, *Admiranda*, III, 3: "velut commune totius terrae opidum"; Lipsius, *Admiranda*, III, 5: "universam Romam miraculum esse."

36   Cf. *ILE* 99 01 03 (= *Cent. Germ.*, 48) to Johannes ab Hollant: "Sed falli te nolo, ubi magnae virtutes, magna item fere vitia aut crebra, et curae iudiciique tui erit bona excerpere, alia spernere ac vitare. Sicut Ulysses ille blandientes, sed insidiantes scopulos surda aure praetervexit, oculos tantum habuit apertos, sic multa tibi illic (atque adeo in reliqua Italia) obiter videnda tantum sunt, non in aures, minus in animum admittenda."

37   *ILE* 99 01 03 (= *Cent. Germ.*, 48) to Johannes ab Hollant: "Iter etiam omne tuum et emansio brevis sit. Biennium si impendis, satis est; ac longior mora oblectare magis potest quam formare."

38   *ILE* I, 78 04 03 (= *Cent. misc. I*, 3): "et haec litterarum studia quiete secretoque magis gaudeant, quam motu aut discursu ... Et de libris quidem, nemo it negatum quin domi habeantur tractenturque melius."

39   *ILE* II, 84 01 05 O: "tamen, ut adolescentia nostra tunc fuit, nec abdita illa et a fronte remota rerum penetravimus, nec cum accuratione satis excerpsimus quidquid faceret ad meliorem usum. Scilicet erravi eundem errorem, quem plerique hodie mihi compares, et pueritiam adolescentiamque peregrinationibus dedi, quae iudicium et dilectum profecto quaerunt, id est, virum."

40   *ILE* XIII, 00 01 02 H (= *Cent. Belg.*, II, 31), to Otho Hartius concerning the education of his son, and *ILE* XIII, 00 12 29 S (= *Cent. Belg.*, I, 61), to his pupil Willem Scarberger.

41   M. Morford, *Stoics and Neostoics: Rubens and the Circle of Lipsius*. Princeton, 1991, p. 33.

42   After Ennius, *Annales*, 390: *moribus antiquis res stat Romana virisque* ("The Roman republic stands by its ancient customs and men"). The verse is quoted by Cicero (*De Republica*, 5, 1) and by St. Augustine (*De civitate Dei*, 2, 21).

43   C. Nativel, 'Juste Lipse antiquaire', in: C. Mouchel (ed.), *Juste Lipse (1547–1606) en son temps*. Paris, 1996, pp. 275–93.

44   This influential topos *Romam in Roma quaerere* can be found as early as Celio Calcagnini (1479–1541). See Tucker, *The Poet's Odyssey*, p. 55. See also footnotes 3 and 24 above.

Colophon

This book has been published to accompany the exhibition 'On the road with Plantin. Travel in the 16th century' at the Museum Plantin-Moretus in Antwerp, from 24 March until 1 August 2021.

'On the road with Plantin' is part of the events programme to commemorate the 500th anniversary of Christophe Plantin's birth.

Exhibition
Project Curators: Vera Nys, Werner van Hoof
Design: Ann Op de Beeck
Travel Photography: Cédric Raskin
Soundscape: Senjan Jansen
Lightshow: Sotesa
Audience Development & Learning: Vera Nys
Paper Conservation and Restoration: Elke Van Herck, Malou Van Peer, Annelies Van den Wijngaert
Exhibition lighting: Louis Prenen
Realization: City Maintenance/Special Assignments, Etoile Mecanique

Book
Final Editing: Werner van Hoof
Authors: Dirk Imhof, Hubert Meeus, Jan Papy, Cédric Raskin, Christophe Schellekens, Gerrit Verhoeven
Editing: Griet Claerhout, Vera Nys
Translation and Editing (English): Guy Shipton
Design: Ann Walkers
Printing: Van Lijsebetten
Publisher: BAI

Thanks to: Nico De Brabander, Jan De Bruyn, Anneleen Decraene, Virginie D'haene, Viviane De Keersmaecker, Samah Doussene, Hassan El Morabet, Jolanta Gwarek, Iris Kockelbergh, Dina Lavrova, Deo Ndayikengurukiye, Mohamad Othman, Kristof Selleslach, Lisette van Erp

Photo Credits: Peter Maes: 28-29, 30, 100 image 7 and 8, 111, 115, 119, Cédric Raskin: 44-73, Other images: collection City of Antwerp, Museum Plantin-Moretus

Alderman for Culture: Nabilla Ait Daoud
Managing Director of Talent Development and Leisure Activities, City of Antwerp: Steven Thielemans
City Heritage and Museum Policy Coordinator, City of Antwerp: Lies Buyse

ISBN 9789085868095
D/2020/5751/08
© 2020 text: BAI and the authors

Unless otherwise provided by law, no part of this publication may be reproduced or duplicated without the written permission of the publisher.

Cover illustration: Map *Germania* from: Abraham Ortelius, *Theatre de l'univers, contenant les cartes de tout le monde avec une brieve declaration d'icelles*. Antwerpen, Ch. Plantin, 1587.